# INTRODUCTION

**PROCEED WITH CAUTION.**

Kindly step this way, or trip this way if Baby Grumpling (he of the strategically positioned banana-skin, worm sandwich and glue-on-the-loo-seat fame) has anything to do with it.

Meet Wellington - bon vivant, wit, raconteur, swordsman, adventurer, but mostly a scruffy schoolkid with the singular distinction of being named after his own footwear. Meet his bone companion - Boot, a wall-to-wall dog who believes he's not a dog at all but the reincarnation of an eighteenth-century nobleman. Meet Maisie, a girl who doubles as a sackful of old Army boots. Meet the love of her life, Marlon - who doesn't double at anything since he's too dim to perform such a complicated mathematical manoeuvre.

Follow them through this their latest collection of adventures and step back into the hilarious world of childhood. Mind you-if your childhood was anything like theirs you will have learned by now to be cautious about stepping back into anything.

*Maurice Dodd.*

W40

W41

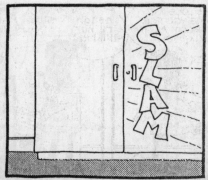

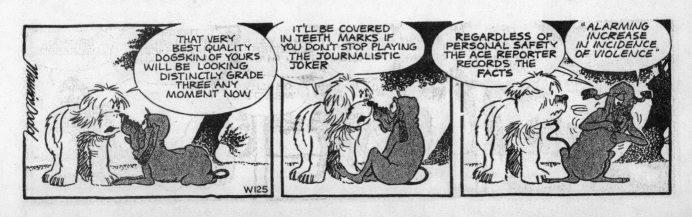

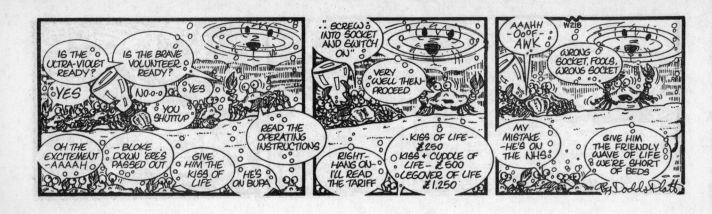

# KEEP A REGULAR DATE WITH

# The Perishers

## EVERY MORNING IN THE DAILY MIRROR

© 1989 Mirror Publications Ltd. First published in Great Britain by Mirror Publications Ltd., 3rd Floor, Greater London House, Hampstead Road, London NW1 7QQ. Printed in Great Britain by Spottiswoode Ballantyne Printers Ltd., Colchester and London. Distributed by IPC Magazines, Circulation Sales and Distribution, London.

The World of

ANDY CAPP

cartoons by

Reg Smythe

# CITIZENSHIP AND THE ENVIRONMENT

**Andrew Dobson**

OXFORD
UNIVERSITY PRESS

# OXFORD

UNIVERSITY PRESS

Great Clarendon Street, Oxford OX2 6DP

Oxford University Press is a department of the University of Oxford.
It furthers the University's objective of excellence in research, scholarship,
and education by publishing worldwide in

Oxford New York

Auckland Bangkok Buenos Aires Cape Town Chennai
Dar es Salaam Delhi Hong Kong Istanbul Karachi Kolkata
Kuala Lumpur Madrid Melbourne Mexico City Mumbai Nairobi
São Paulo Shanghai Taipei Tokyo Toronto

Oxford is a registered trade mark of Oxford University Press
in the UK and in certain other countries

Published in the United States
by Oxford University Press Inc., New York

British Library Cataloguing in Publication Data
Data available

Library of Congress Cataloging in Publication Data
Data available
ISBN 0-19-925843-0
ISBN 0-19-925844-9 (pbk.)

1 3 5 7 9 10 8 6 4 2

Typeset by Newgen Imaging Systems (P) Ltd., Chennai, India
Printed in Great Britain
on acid-free paper by
Biddles Ltd., Guildford and King's Lynn

*For Concha, Patrick, and Carla*

# Contents

# Contents

# Acknowledgements

I have given papers on topics in this book at the following places, and I am grateful to participants for their guidance: Birmingham University, Dundee University, Reading University, Nottingham University, London School of Economics, Luleå University of Technology, Universidad de Valencia, Keele University, Open University, Universidad de Santiago de Compostela, Learning and Skills Development Agency. A number of my friends and colleagues have been burdened by reading my work and I thank the following especially: Robert Barrett, John Barry, Mark Beard, Derek Bell, Margaret Canovan, Robyn Eckersley, Cecile Fabre, John Horton, Ken Jones, Rosemary O'Kane, Raia Prokhovnik, Angel Rivero, Mike Saward, Piers Stephens, Hidemi Suganani, Angel Valencia, Rob Walker, and Marcel Wissenburg. Most of them will recognize my attempts to deal with objections they raised and suggestions they made, but none of them is likely to be fully satisfied. Some of them, indeed, pointed towards work that lies beyond the scope of this book — or at least I take temporary refuge in that thought. Thanks to Fran Ford, too, for helping me through my first year at the Open University, and to Dominic Byatt at Oxford University Press for his sympathetic editing.

Andrew Dobson
*Open University, Milton Keynes*
*January 2003*

# Introduction

There is a European Union directive that calls for deep cuts in the amount of household waste sent to landfill sites in Britain—currently about 1400 of them. 'The EU Landfill Directive requires the UK to reduce the volume of biodegradable municipal waste sent to landfill by 2010, with further reductions in 2013 and 2020. Failure to meet these targets could result in fines of up to £180 million per year' (Strategy Unit 2002: 9). This leaves the British government with the tricky task of working out how best to wean the public and its institutions off the habit of throwing stuff away. Downing Street has a Strategy Unit charged with suggesting answers to such questions, and in November 2001 Margaret Beckett, Secretary of State for the Environment, Food, and Rural Affairs, announced a 'Strategy Unit Waste study', to be completed within a year. The Unit's proposals shed interesting light on the prevailing view of how to get people to do environmentally beneficial things when their inclination is not to do them.

The report notes that household waste is growing at 3 per cent annually—faster than GDP—and the authors wonder why (Strategy Unit 2002: 8). The answer offered is that 'there are few financial incentives in place for either industry or householders to seek alternatives to landfill' (Strategy Unit 2002: 8). With this premise established, the solution to the problem is obvious and the report predictably recommends 'Greater freedom for local authorities to develop new financial incentives for householders to reduce and recycle their waste. Householders currently pay the same Council Tax no matter how much waste they produce or whether they recycle or not. This means that they have no incentive to manage their waste in more sustainable ways' (Strategy Unit 2002: 13). A concrete suggestion floated in the summer of 2002 was to charge people for taking over-quota sacks of rubbish away—say £1.00 (€0.6) per sack, or £5.00 (€3.0) per month.

From one point of view the logic is impeccable: people will want to avoid paying the rubbish tax and so will reduce the amount of waste they throw away. The proposal is rooted in the 'self-interested rational actor' model of human motivation, according to which people do things either for some gain or to avoid some harm to themselves. Critics of the proposed scheme immediately pointed out that this model contains the seeds of its own demise. People uncommitted to the idea behind the scheme will take the line of least resistance in a way entirely consistent with the model of behaviour on which the scheme depends, but entirely at odds with its desired outcomes. As a *Guardian* newspaper leader pointed out, 'Rather than pay up, the public are likely to vote with their cars and take their rubbish and dump it on the pavement, in the countryside or in someone else's backyard' (12 July 2002).

Supporters of the financial incentive route to sustainability will claim, though, that it works and that there is plenty of evidence to prove it. They will point, for example, to the road-pricing scheme that has been operating in a part of the ancient English city of Durham for the past few months (I write in January 2003). It costs £2.00 (€1.20) to take your car into the square at the top of the city, and it was hoped that this would cut traffic by 50 per cent within a year. In fact it has been cut by

90 per cent in just a few months. This is success beyond the planners' wildest dreams.

Imagine, though, that the scheme was withdrawn tomorrow. No doubt some people would continue to take the bus into town, or to cycle or walk, having seen what a difference there is between a square empty of cars and one that is filled with them. But the Italian experience of car-less city days suggests that when cars are allowed back in, people fire up their engines and drive into town. The chances are that traffic levels would return to their pre-fine levels within a few weeks or months. The 'success' of the Durham scheme, then, is bought at the cost of the signal failure to make anything other than a superficial impression on people's habits and practices. The change in behaviour lasts only as long as the incentives or disincentives are in place—and these are inevitably subject to the vagaries of fashion, experiment, and the direction of the political wind that happens to be blowing at the time.

At no point in this debate was an alternative approach canvassed, admirably captured in the following from Ludwig Beckman:

the fact that the sustainability of the consumerist and individualist lifestyle is put in question undoubtedly raises a whole range of questions about how to reconstruct our society. What new economic and political institutions are needed? What regulations and set of incentives are necessary in order to redirect patterns of behaviour in sustainable directions?

However, the question of sustainable behaviour cannot be reduced to a discussion about balancing carrots and sticks. The citizen that sorts her garbage or that prefers ecological goods will often do this because she feels committed to ecological values and ends. The citizen may not, that is, act in sustainable ways solely out of economic or practical incentives: people sometimes choose to do good for other reasons than fear (of punishment or loss) or desire (for economic rewards or social status). People sometimes do good because they want to be virtuous. (Beckman 2001: 179)

Beckman is gesturing here towards a conception of environmental or ecological citizenship, and that is what this book is about. Financial penalties invite attempts to get around them, as in the temptation to purchase means of making number plates illegible to cameras as cars enter the Congestion Charging Zone in the centre of London. Consumers react to superficial signals without caring about, understanding, or being committed to the underlying rationale for the incentives to which they respond. Ecological citizens, on the other hand, would harbour a commitment to the principles and would 'do good' because it is the right thing to do.

In one sense, then, this book is a contribution to the debate about how to achieve a sustainable society. I do not regard ecological citizenship (which I shall distinguish from environmental citizenship in Chapter 3) as *the* answer to this question, but I do regard it as an underexplored one. I do not even regard it as a complete alternative to the dis/incentives route sketched above, since such instruments will almost certainly be a part of the policy toolkit for sustainability, particularly in the context of private corporations. For a number of reasons, though (some of which I look at in Chapter 2), citizenship has made a palpable comeback in recent years. It is now commonplace to find it used to articulate political projects across the political spectrum, and a considerable amount of intellectual effort has been devoted to positioning those projects in the complex conceptual field that citizenship has become. In contrast to this, no systematic attempt has been made to relate the themes of ecological politics to those of citizenship (again, I shall discuss what work there is in Chapter 3). This is surprising, given that since its contemporary re-emergence, ecological politics has been habitually associated with citizenship-sounding issues such as the reinvigoration of the public sphere, the commitment to political participation, and the sense that individuals can make a political difference.

On the other hand, though, some aspects of the political–ecological project seem to lie outside the discursive territory of citizenship. For one, we know that environmental problems do not confine themselves neatly to the boundaries of nation-states, yet citizenship is most often thought of precisely in terms of those boundaries. Can the language of citizenship be enlisted beyond the state? What, in other words, is the 'citizenship-space' of ecological politics? Is cosmopolitan citizenship of any help? Similarly, while we are used to thinking of citizenship in terms of rights and obligations, the former are increasingly regarded as being 'earned' by the dutiful exercise of the latter (e.g. 'workfare' schemes). Some of the obligations of the putative ecological citizen, though, seem inappropriately expressed in this language of reciprocity (we are not all equally responsible for environmental degradation). Does this mean that ecological politics cannot be discussed or pursued in terms of citizenship? Again, citizenship is almost always regarded as belonging to the public arena, yet ecological politics is a politics of everyday life and it involves private as well as public spaces. Is citizenship therefore an inappropriate vehicle for greens to travel in? Is composting in your garden an act of citizenship or not?

These brief remarks will be enough to show that political ecologists cannot uncomplicatedly occupy the discursive territory of citizenship. The first two chapters of this book are, therefore, devoted to discussing aspects of the contemporary context of citizenship (Chapter 1), and developing a type of citizenship that I call post-cosmopolitan (Chapter 2), which I believe to be called for by that contemporary context, and which cannot be expressed in either the dominant liberal or civic–republican form of citizenship. I see these two chapters as contributing to contemporary debates on citizenship, irrespective of the environmental implications they may have.

Chapter 3 develops ecological citizenship as a specific instantiation and interpretation of post-cosmopolitan citizenship, and I take the opportunity to draw a distinction between environmental and ecological citizenship. I am more intellectually interested in the latter, although I do not see them as political alternatives. Both of them are key to progressing towards a sustainable society. This book is mostly about environmental and ecological citizenship in the context of so-called advanced, broadly liberal–democratic societies, and so in Chapter 4, I discuss the ideological difficulties of instantiating ecological citizenship in such societies. The issue with which I grapple here is that the putative 'value-neutrality' of the liberal state makes it unsuitable as a sponsor of the idea and practice of sustainability which appears so obviously driven by a 'comprehensive doctrine' as to how the 'good life' should be lived. I eschew the two standard ripostes to this argument. The first is that liberal states are not actually value-neutral, so why shouldn't they endorse the sustainability version of non-neutrality? The second is that sustainability is not a matter of values, but of science, so liberal states will have no trouble adopting the path of sustainability once it has been scientifically determined just where the path is. My alternative is to offer an 'immanent critique' of liberal state neutrality and to show how, in the case of sustainability at least, living up to its value-neutral billing will involve it in full-body value immersion and the endorsement (perhaps counter-intuitively) of so-called 'strong' versions of sustainability.

Any discussion of citizenship eventually confronts the question of where citizens are going to come from, and this is especially true in the ecological context where they seem to be in such short supply. In Chapter 5, I broach just one type of answer to this question—citizenship education. What I offer is a discursive case study of the English experience. This seems appropriate because citizenship education has only just become a statutory requirement (as of August 2002) in secondary (or high) schools in England, and so the syllabus has pretty much been designed from scratch. I ask whether this syllabus offers the opportunity to teach ecological citizenship, as described in Chapter 3, and whether, following Chapter 4, this can be done effectively in state-sponsored schools in the liberal context. I come to broadly optimistic conclusions—in this particular context at least—but with the caveat that the Trojan Horse with which the British government has provided teachers has to be occupied and driven in the right direction for it to make a difference.

The government hopes that citizenship classes will improve the quality of democracy—or at least that they will get more people to representative democracy's first base: the polling booth. I see ecological citizenship as improving democracy's chances of producing sustainable outcomes. Much green political theory over the past few years has been devoted to discussing the relationship between democracy and sustainability, largely in response to the accusation that sustainability inevitably entails degrees of authoritarianism since people will not voluntarily make the changes that sustainability requires. The vast majority of contributors to this debate have converged on 'discursive democracy' as offering the best chance of enabling democratic procedures to result in sustainable outcomes. This is because discursive democracy entails not only the registering of people's preferences in the decision-making process, but also the possibility that those preferences be revised as a result of debate and discussion. Once the ecological point is made, in other words, the idea is that people will see how good it is and consequently come round to sustainable ways of thinking and acting. At best, though, the jury is out on this. Graham Smith, who has done more work than most on this question, writes that, 'if we are looking for decisive evidence that the institutionalization of deliberation will lead to the greening of liberal democracies and, in particular, the emergence of an environmentally enlightened citizenry, we will be disappointed. The evidence is no more than suggestive' (Smith 2004: forthcoming).

In late 2000, Europe was rocked by protests about the high price of petrol (gas for cars, trucks, and lorries), and in Britain the government backed away from increased taxation because of the picketing of oil refineries and the generally high level of anger among the public. Barry Holden notes that the government failed to make the environmental case for high petrol prices and comments that, 'This is not to say that the environmental case would necessarily have won the day. But it is to suggest that it may have done so, had it been put' (Holden 2002: 76). It was indeed extraordinary that a government that had loudly trumpeted its commitment to the environment during the General Election failed to take this golden opportunity to make the environmental case for higher petrol prices. But the rub, in any case, is that the introduction of the environmental point into the debate only 'may' have won the day. There are no guarantees anywhere, of course, but democracy might be given a little shove towards sustainability by getting environmental concern in at the ground level. People are the 'raw material' of the democratic process and what they think and do makes a difference to the process's outcomes—if we do not believe that, then why endorse democratic procedures in the first place? My view is that ecological citizens will make democracies more responsive to sustainability demands than consumers charged a pound, a euro, a dollar, or 100 yen to have an extra bag of rubbish taken away. One by one, then, the signposts to sustainability are being erected and I regard ecological citizenship as a key addition to the collection.

# Chapter 1

# Towards Post-cosmopolitanism

Cosmopolitanism and globalization play a central role in my articulation of ecological citizenship, but since they are such contested terms it is important for me to make clear what I understand by them. Moreover, given that I believe that the most commonly cited understandings of them are inadequate to the task of developing a notion of ecological citizenship, I shall not simply be choosing between definitions, but rather reconstructing them. In this chapter, then, I offer a critique of particular understandings of both globalization and cosmopolitanism, and show how my asymmetrical understanding of the former leads to a critique of both 'dialogic' and 'distributive' forms of the latter. This critique, in turn, produces the post-cosmopolitanism that I carry forward into Chapter 2 in the explicit context of citizenship.

The view of globalization that I think we should reject is couched in terms of the interdependence and interconnectedness of states in the post-Westphalian, globalizing world. The language of 'interdependence' implies a rough parity of cause and effect as states make their way through a globalizing world, 'negotiating' for advantage where possible, but with such negotiations undergirded by the recognition that no state can expect to isolate itself from the more or less reciprocal effects of other states. Some will object that 'interdependence' does not imply a rough parity at all and that it simply denotes a relationship. I am prepared to concede that the relationship between a master and slave, for example, can be described as one of 'interdependence', but I hope that it will be conceded in return that this description completely misses the characteristic that best enables us to understand the nature of the relationship—its inequality.

## Globalization and 'Interconnectedness'

In one of his most recent articulations of globalization, David Held argues that it possesses four features:

First, it involves a stretching of social, political and economic activities across political frontiers, regions and continents ... second, globalization is marked by the growing magnitude of networks and flows of trade, investment, finance, culture and so on. Third, globalization can be linked to a speeding up of global interactions and processes, as the evolution of world-wide systems of transport and communication increases the velocity of the diffusion of ideas, goods, information, capital and people. And, fourth, it involves the deepening impact of global interactions and processes such that the effects of distant events can be highly significant and even the most local developments can come to have enormous global consequences. In this particular sense, the boundaries between domestic matters and global affairs become fuzzy. In short, globalization can be thought of as the widening, intensifying, speeding up and growing impact of world-wide interconnectedness. (Held 2002: 60–1)

Let me stress that this brief paragraph does not reflect every-thing Held has ever written about globalization, and so what follows should be taken to refer to the *animus* that informs this description, rather than a critique of Held *in toto*. I do believe, though, that the language used here is widely employed in descriptions of globalization and that it repays some attention since it accurately captures, represents, and above all reproduces the 'interdependence' view of globalization that currently dom-inates political debate. Let us take three of the features that Held identifies one by one.

First he refers to a 'stretching' of activities across forms of political, social, and even geographical space that we previously thought, perhaps, to constitute boundaries to such activities. Leaving aside the objection that this stretching has been a con-stant feature of social and economic history, especially in times of empire, the language of stretching puts us in mind of the expansion of a balloon in which the surface area of the balloon expands at an equal rate on every part of its surface simultan-eously. I shall come back to the shortcomings of this way of expressing one of the features of globalization when we have considered the alternative view.

Second, Held talks of a 'growing magnitude of networks and flows of trade, investment, finance, culture and so on'. Once again, the language of 'networks' and 'flows' expresses a quite specific political imaginary, in which political actors of all types (and no distinction is drawn here between them) are nodes in an interconnecting lattice, between which goods, money, and people 'flow' in ways and directions determined by the undifferentiated 'stretching' outlined in the first feature. Again I shall return to networks and flows shortly.

Third, Held refers to the way in which globalization involves a collapse of space, such that events that are distant from the observer can have a significant impact, seemingly dispropor-tionate to the distance at which it has occurred. The boundaries between the 'domestic' and the 'global' become 'fuzzy', and all

11

this (I mean this collapse of space and the other two features on which Held has commented) is expressed in the trope that dominates this particular articulation of globalization—that of 'world-wide interconnectedness'.

## A Critique of 'Interconnectedness'

What is missing from this description of globalization is the asymmetry at work in it. 'Political communities', Held writes, 'are enmeshed and entrenched in complex structures of over-lapping forces, processes and movements' (2002: 61). It is easy to overdo the complexity and especially easy to overdo the overlapping. Compare the Held view with the following from the Indian environmentalist Vandana Shiva:

The 'global' in the dominant discourse is the political space in which a particular dominant local seeks global control, and frees itself of local, national and international restraints. The global does not represent the universal human interest, it represents a particular local and parochial interest which has been globalized through the scope of its reach. The seven most powerful countries, the G-7, dictate global affairs, but the interests that guide them remain narrow, local and parochial. (Shiva 1998: 231)

Held talks, it will be remembered, of the blurring of boundaries between domestic and global affairs. Shiva's point is that not everyone touched by this blurring experiences it in the same way. Held tells us that 'the effects of distant events can be highly significant and even the most local developments can come to have enormous global consequences'. Shiva's crucial corrective is that only the 'local developments' of countries or other agen-cies with globalizing possibilities have global consequences. She puts it like this:

The notion of 'global' facilitates this skewed view of a common future. The construction of the global environment narrows the South's options while increasing the North's. Through its global reach, the North exists in the South, but the South exists only within itself, since it has no global reach. Thus the South can *only* exist locally, while only the North exists globally.                    (Shiva 1998: 233)

Globalization is, on this reading, an asymmetrical process in which not only its fruits are divided up unequally, but also in which the very possibility of 'being global' is unbalanced. It is not that Held's position is incompatible with Shiva's corrective, but that *beginning* with asymmetry rather than *adding it on* makes a considerable difference to the political prescriptions that follow the description. This should become clearer as the chapter develops, but let me indicate in a little more detail the effect of Shiva's view on Held's gloss.

First, the metaphor of 'stretching' fails to capture the way in which the social, political, and economic activities to which he refers cross boundaries in one direction only. It is truer than it ever was that 'if America sneezes the rest of the world catches a cold', but Bangladesh can contract viral pneumonia without it making the slightest difference to the United States. The South, as Shiva says, can only exist locally, and the direction of travel of globalization is generally from the powerful to the powerless.

Second, to describe the movement of 'trade, investment, finance, [and] culture' in terms of 'networks' and 'flows', as Held does, is in effect to misdescribe them in the same way that to describe the relationship between master and slave as 'interdependent' is to misdescribe it. As an example of the way the global terms of negotiation are skewed, consider the manner in which the World Trade Organization (WTO) operates. The WTO denies skewing because, it says, the organization's decisions are taken by consensus. This is much more equitable than a simple majority system of voting, says the WTO, since even the smallest and least powerful participant in negotiations can oppose an agreement through using what is effectively the power of veto. The reality, though, is somewhat different: consensus

**13**

decision-making only works in the way the WTO suggests when all participants are equally powerful. As the WTO itself recognizes, though, 'not every country has the same bargaining power'. In cases where governments refuse to come on board, the WTO continues by saying, rather darkly, that 'reluctant countries are persuaded by being offered something in return'. The key orientating question here is: in a world of asymmetrical globalization, what can be offered to countries that already have most of what they want? What can one offer the present United States, for example, if it refuses to play ball with everyone else? The answer, in effect, is nothing. Pre-eminently powerful countries do not have to think in terms of bargaining, of partnerships. In sum, to describe the WTO as if it were a 'node' in a 'network' of multilateral 'flows' of 'trade, investment, and finance' is to speak of globalization in terms of characteristics that we might *want* it to possess rather than those it actually *does* possess.

A third feature of globalization, for Held, is the 'increased velocity of the diffusion of ideas, goods, information, capital and people'. Held omits, here, to point out that most of this diffusion is in one direction only—to such an extent, indeed, that 'diffusion', with its multi-directional sense, is the wrong word to describe the phenomenon. Take the movement of people, for example. For some, space seems almost to have been erased altogether, as the means of traversing it (physically and virtually) become ever more rapid and 'at-hand'. For others, space is what encloses them—thick, material, resistant. The former 'diffuse', and the latter can only 'refuse'—and often not even that. Zygmunt Bauman's view of the 'people question' under globalization is surely nearer the mark than David Held's:

Like all other known societies, the postmodern, consumer society is a stratified one. But it is possible to tell one kind of society from another by the dimensions along which it stratifies its members. The dimension along which those 'high up' and 'low down' are plotted in a society of consumers, is their *degree of mobility*—their freedom to choose where to be.                                    (Bauman 1998: 86)

In Bauman's globalization there is a first and a second world, the inhabitants of which are distinguished by their ability to traverse space as and when they wish:

For the inhabitants of the first world—the increasingly cosmopolitan, extraterritorial world of global businessmen, global culture managers or global academics, state borders are levelled down, as they are dismantled for the world's commodities, capital and finances. For the inhabitant of the second world, the walls built of immigration controls, of residence laws and of 'clean streets' and 'zero tolerance' policies, grow taller; the moats separating them from the sites of their desire and of dreamed-of redemption grow deeper, while all bridges, at the first attempt to cross them prove to be drawbridges. The first travel at will, get much fun from their travel (particularly if travelling first class or using private aircraft), are cajoled or bribed to travel and welcomed with smiles and open arms when they do. The second travel surreptitiously, often illegally, sometimes paying more for the crowded steerage of a stinking unseaworthy boat than others pay for business-class gilded luxuries—and are frowned upon, and, if unlucky, arrested and promptly deported, when they arrive.          (Bauman 1998: 89)

This is not the 'diffusion' of 'ideas, goods, information, capital, and people', but their *transfusion*, and it is mostly one way. Even the occasional phenomenon that looks as though it is moving in the other direction turns out to be expressed in terms of Bauman's first world political and cultural space—think Bollywood, for example.

So deep are the moats and so high are the walls that separate the movers from the stayers, and so accustomed are we to seeing these barriers stand firm, that we are astonished when they are breached. This is one of the lasting truths of the attack on New York's Twin Towers in September 2001, captured in the closing lines of Millennium Poet Simon Armitage's poem, 'The Convergence of the Twain':

> VI
> With hindsight now we track
> the vapour-trail of each flight-path

arcing through blue morning, like a curved
thought.

VII
And in retrospect plot
the weird prospect
of a passenger plane beading on an office-block.

VIII
But long before that dawn,
with those towers drawing
in worth and name to their full height, an
opposite was forming.

IX
a force still years and miles off,
yet moving headlong forwards, locked on a
collision course.

X
Then time and space
contracted, so whatever distance
held those worlds apart thinned to an instant.

XI
During which, cameras framed
moments of grace
before the furious contact wherein earth and
heaven fused.                          (Armitage 2002,
                                  Faber and Faber Ltd.)

The contraction of time and space recorded in stanza X is a
commonplace for the first world, but its visitation *upon* the first
world in such a dramatic fashion is, to date, a unique experience. This was an underhand breaching of the first law of
globalization: travel is permitted in one direction only.

The final feature of Held's view of globalization, it will
be remembered, involves the arresting thought that 'the
deepening impact of global interactions and processes' means
that 'the effects of distant events can be highly significant
and even the most local developments can come to have

enormous global consequences'. I have already pointed out Shiva's response to this, and it seems to me to be the right one. Her argument is that while some countries can be local *and* global, most can only ever be local: 'Through its global reach, the North exists in the South, but the South exists only within itself, since it has no global reach. Thus the South can *only* exist locally, while only the North exists globally' (Shiva 1998: 233). Bauman offers a sonorous echo of this thought:

Alongside the emerging planetary dimensions of business, finance, trade and information flow, a 'localizing', space-fixing process is set in motion. Between them, the two closely inter-connected processes sharply differentiate the existential conditions of whole populations and of various segments of each one of the populations. What appears as globalization for some means localization for others; signalling a new freedom for some, upon many others it descends as an uninvited and cruel fate . . . the effects of that new condition are radically unequal. Some of us become fully and truly 'global'; some are fixed in their 'locality'—a predicament neither pleasurable nor endurable in the world in which the 'globals' set the tone and compose the rules of the life-game.                    (Bauman 1998: 2)

As it happens, environmental politics is an excellent example—especially in the guise of global warming—of the nature of asymmetrical globalization. Think for a moment of the ideal structure for a medium or a phenomenon through which to 'turn local language into global grammar'. There must be a local 'view' of it, of course, but equally evidently this local view must be translatable into global effects. It must, in other words, be 'globalizable'. Even more ideally, enacting the local view locally should have immediate and constant global effects, such that every enactment of the local view is always simultaneously (or 'always already', in the postmodern idiom) an act of globalization. Can there possibly be a medium and a phenomenon that live up to such exacting standards? Indeed there can: the environment is the medium and global warming is the phenomenon. To explain.

In November 2001 a key stage of the Kyoto protocol on climate change was negotiated in Marrakech. It is now common knowledge that the aim of the protocol was, and is, to limit the emissions of the six gases that are most clearly responsible for global warming. The outcome of the talks in Marrakech came nowhere near to satisfying the demands of the environmental movement—nor, indeed, of the International Panel on Climate Change, which recommends a 60 per cent cut in 1990 greenhouse gas emissions by 2012. The Kyoto protocol, even if fully adhered to, will only produce a 5.2 per cent cut, delaying warming that would have occurred in 2094–2100—just a 6-year respite. Despite the relatively feeble nature of the agreement, of the thirty-nine countries that started out on the long road from Kyoto in 1997, only thirty-eight reached Marrakech in 2001. The one that dropped out was the United States. Despite the fact that the United States with just 5 per cent of the world's population produces a quarter of the world's greenhouse gases, 11 times as much per head of population as China, 20 times more than India, and 300 times more than Mozambique—despite all this, the United States claims that the Kyoto protocol is 'unfair', since it exempts developing countries and is against the United States' best economic interests.

It is commonly argued that in withdrawing from the Kyoto protocol the Bush administration was simply returning favours accrued during his first presidential election campaign, to which various oil, coal, gas, and utility companies contributed some $50 m. These connections and favours surely are linked to America's withdrawal from the Kyoto protocol negotiations. But they also represent a way of life, a way of life it is impossible to pursue without 'always already' affecting people in other parts of the planet. In explaining his rejection of the Kyoto protocol, George W. Bush said that 'a growing population requires more energy to heat and cool our homes, more gas to drive our cars' (Bush 2001). Bush would like to present this as a statement of fact, but it is, rather, a prospectus for a way of life. 'Heat our homes' (rather than an extra layer of clothing); 'cool our homes' (rather than open the window); 'more gas' (rather than reduce fuel consumption); 'to drive our cars' (rather than get about less, or in a different way). This local prospectus, in turn, has immediate global effects in its contribution to global warming. I do not intend to demonize the United States with these remarks. This is an example, rather, of the way in which asymmetrical globalization operates, and the process is repeated daily in untold numbers and less spectacular manifestations by each and every agent with a globalizing capacity.

In sum, as long as we conceive globalization in the seductive, undifferentiated terms of networks, processes, and interdependences, we will fail to make its divisive, stratifying, and unequal aspects sufficiently central to our understanding of the phenomenon. The key thing to bear in mind is that 'There is polarization in the distribution of wealth at the global level, differential evolution of intracountry income inequality, and substantial growth of poverty and misery in the world at large, and in most countries, both developed and developing' (Castells 2001: 352). In more detail:

In a global approach, there has been, over the past three decades, increasing inequality and polarization in the distribution of wealth. According to UNDP's 1996 Human Development Report, in 1993 only US$5 trillion of the US$23 trillion global GDP were from the developing countries even if they accounted for nearly 80 percent of total population. The poorest 20 percent of the world's people have seen their share of global income decline from 2.3 percent to 1.4 percent in the past 30 years. Meanwhile, the share of the richest 20 percent has risen from 70 percent to 85 percent. This doubled the ratio of the share of the richest over the poorest—from 30:1 to 61:1. (Castells 2001: 351)

These details are sufficient to show why the language of 'sharing and negotiating' used by Held to describe globalization ('political power is shared and negotiated among diverse forces and agencies at many levels, from the local to the global'; (Held 2002: 62)) is inadequate to the task. Let me stress again that I have no reason to think that Held would challenge Castells' data; all the more reason, then, to query the cognitive dissonance between the asymmetries and inequalities that the data implies, and Held's own gloss on the dynamics at work in globalization with which I began this chapter. In this context it is unfortunate for Held, yet symptomatic of the shortcomings of his gloss on globalization, that he should choose the Kyoto negotiations as an example of the 'co-ordinated multilateral action' that he regards as a symptomatic and laudable aspect of the process of globalization (Held 2002: 62). We now know that the unilateral decision of the United States to withdraw from the Kyoto agreement on greenhouse gas emissions is far more significant for the global climate than the multilateral negotiations that led to the agreement in the first place. In this sense globalization is an opportunity to be grasped, by those willing and able to do so, to turn local practices into global frameworks.

It will be objected, as I have suggested, that the 'interconnectedness' or 'interdependence' view of globalization is perfectly compatible with an asymmetrical understanding of the global system. On this reading, interconnectedness is taken to denote only the way in which the 'international' is being replaced by the 'global', and once this thought is established then power differentials among the various actors come into descriptive play, and the relevant asymmetries emerge. This view does indeed contrast with a wholly naïve description of the process of globalization which begins and ends with a notion of interdependence from which power is more or less completely absent. David Held does not, of course, subscribe to this naïve view. But there is still a difference, I maintain, between a view in which power is 'added on', and one in which it is constitutive of the description. It would be very hard, I think, to find a paragraph on globalization in the work of Shiva or Bauman, say, like that with which I began the 'Globalization and "Interconnectedness"' section. And this is a difference that makes a difference, because viewing globalization as constitutively asymmetrical makes clearer the nature and direction of the political obligations it entails. For the cosmopolitanism that builds on the interconnectedness view of globalization, the first virtue is often 'equal and open dialogue'. From a materialist asymmetrical point of view, the first virtue is 'more justice'. Again, in interdependence descriptions of globalization, the language of reciprocity bulks large, yet the Shiva view, that some states and agents are globalizing while some are globalized, implies that the former shoulder greater burdens of obligation than the latter. I shall say more about this towards the end of this chapter, and much more about it in the next.

Globalization can be presented, of course, as an opportunity to resist the asymmetries that are present in its actually existing manifestation. The form of resistance I want to discuss here goes by the name of 'cosmopolitanism'. I am aware that cosmopolitanism is a complex and contested term (e.g. Cheah and Robbins 1998; Linklater 1998a; Jones 1999; Breckenridge *et al.* 2002) and I do not pretend a comprehensive account here. I shall refer to two types of cosmopolitanism, which I call respectively 'dialogic' and 'distributive' cosmopolitanism. I have more sympathy with the intentions of the latter of these in that its focus is more firmly on justice as well as on dialogue, and this is key to developing a robust notion of citizenship beyond the state. Its drawback, though, is that in providing principles for redistribution it forgets that we also need reasons for action, and I do not believe that its 'thin' account of the ties that bind— which it shares with dialogic cosmopolitanism—constitute politically compelling reasons. This is especially important if we wish to develop an action-orientated notion of citizenship beyond the state, as I do. I then sketch the theory of obligation that lies at the heart of what I call post-cosmopolitanism, building on both distributive cosmopolitanism and the asymmetrical understanding of globalization I have developed so far.

## *A Critique of Dialogic Cosmopolitanism: Less Dialogue, More Justice*

For Held, 'current cosmopolitanism . . . seems to explicate, and offer a compelling elucidation of, the classical conception of belonging to the human community first and foremost, and the Kantian conception of subjecting all beliefs, relations and practices to the test of whether or not they allow open-ended interaction, uncoerced agreement and impartial judgement' (Held 2002: 64). My most general objection to this type of cosmopolitanism takes the form of the injunction: don't start from here. Just as interdependence globalization begins from the wrong descriptive premises, so this cosmopolitanism looks to the wrong form of community ('the human community'), the wrong modus operandi ('impartiality'), and the wrong political objective (more dialogue and democracy). We should instead be focusing on the specific communities of obligation—or 'obligation spaces'—produced by acts of 'globalization' (i.e. local acts with global consequences); we should recognize that these are communities of injustice first, and only of coerced dialogue second; that the remedy is therefore more justice as well as more democracy; and that partiality is crucial to doing effective justice. I shall try to flesh all this out in what follows.

Let me begin with the nature of dialogic cosmopolitanism's political community. Andrew Linklater, an articulate exponent of the promise of this type of cosmopolitanism, says that he is interested in 'the social bonds which unite and separate, associate and disassociate' (Linklater 1998*a*: 2). He points out that, 'with the rise of the nation-state, one identity was singled out and made central to modern political life. Shared national identity was deemed to be the crucial social bond which links citizens together in the ideal political community' (Linklater 1998a: 179), and he wants to resist the apparently ineluctable linking of 'political community' with the state. Thus: 'Regard for the interests of outsiders can wax in one epoch and wane in another: hence the importance of a cosmopolitan ethic which questions the precise moral significance of national boundaries' (Linklater 1998a: 2). Note, in passing, the slippage from 'political' to 'moral', since this will come to be important later on (it is this cosmopolitanism's mistake, I think, to confuse the moral community with the political community), but otherwise let us share Linklater's determination to seek political communities beyond the state.

Linklater offers us two kinds of social bond beyond the state. The first kind of glue that might hold people together, he says, is a 'commitment to open dialogue': 'the bond which unites them [members of a society] can owe as much to the ethical commitment to open dialogue as to a sense of primordial attachments' (Linklater 1998a: 7). The political task of the cosmopolitan, then, is to 'create institutional frameworks which widen the boundaries of the dialogic community' (Linklater 1998a: 7). The most common criticism of this kind of thing is that it requires too much of a suspension of disbelief; that 'commitment to open dialogue' is a hopelessly weak candidate for social glue-dom in comparison with the 'primordial attachments' of family, history, and culture. My criticism takes a different form, though—the form of a question. The question is: *what will 'open dialogue' tell us that we do not already know?* Dialogic cosmopolitanism's support for open and uncoerced dialogue is clearly aimed at listening to what Linklater and others call 'subaltern voices'—the voices of the dispossessed, the marginalized, the excluded. The cosmopolitan call for more dialogue is so central to its programme that one could be forgiven for thinking that the dispossessed, the marginalized, and the excluded were totally silent. Yet they are not. We know, at least, that they are dispossessed, marginalized, and excluded (by our own lights at any rate), otherwise they would not be so designated.

And we have plenty of specific instances to hand. We know, for example, that two islands that were part of the Pacific nation of Kiribati have disappeared (Environmental News Network 1999) as sea levels have risen, and we know with a fair degree of certainty that some of this sea level rise is caused by global warming. We also know that the Alliance of Small Island States was formed to give voice, among other things, to these states' concerns regarding the effects of global warming on almost forty island states threatened by it. The dialogue in which they are engaged (e.g. their appearances before the United Nations General Assembly) may not be as 'free and uncoerced' as dialogic cosmopolitans might want, but it has been free and uncoerced enough for the Small Island States to be able to tell us that, as far as mitigating global warming is concerned, they believe action should be guided by the principle of 'common but differentiated responsibility' (Alliance of Small Island States n.d.). This principle is based on the recognition that some countries contribute more to global warming than others, and therefore shoulder a bigger responsibility for doing something about it. This stands in stark contrast to George W. Bush's view that it is everyone's responsibility: 'This is a challenge that requires a 100 percent effort; ours, and the rest of the world's' (Bush 2001). The Small Island States' view of the appropriate pattern of obligation in the global warming context is a good example of the non-reciprocal nature of obligation that I believe is implied by an asymmetrically globalizing world. It would be odd, to say the least, to claim that inhabitants of the Small Island States (excepting those few who make a net contribution to global warming) have $CO_2$-based obligations to me, for example. Yet Bush's 'shared reciprocity' flows more obviously and seamlessly from the interdependence view of globalization.

It is hard to see, in sum, what more dialogue will tell us beyond these already contrasting and rather clear positions. The cosmopolitan focus on dialogue leads Linklater to suggest that 'A just society is one which "recognises and allows all participants to have a voice, to narrate from their own perspective"' (Linklater 1998*a*: 96). But the Small Island States do not want to talk any more. What they want is for net contributors to global warming to reduce their impact on the global environment.

The sense that the right strategy is to make do with what we have already got, in terms of discursive positions, is implicitly present in dialogic cosmopolitanism's own recognition that getting in all potential information is impossible anyway: 'The stress on the voice of the other highlights the difficulty (and ultimately the impossibility) of entering into pure dialogic relations in which only the force of the better argument prevails. Dialogic communities can never be confident that all the barriers to open discourse have been removed' (Linklater 1998*a*: 99). Yet the normative cosmopolitan focus on dialogue is so determining that, like those toys with round bottoms that can never be knocked over, it always comes bouncing back. So Linklater says: 'If societies were largely self-contained and incapable of doing harm to one another then the boundaries of moral communities could converge with the boundaries of actual political communities, but the reality is quite different and societies are inevitably drawn into complex dialogues about the principles of international coexistence' (Linklater 1998*a*: 85). The jump from 'harm' to 'dialogue' is significant. Why not to redistributive or restorative justice?

Once again, something like my own position is already present in Linklater's own presentation of cosmopolitanism, as in the following: 'the primary duty of protecting the vulnerable rests with the source of transnational harm and not with the national governments of the victims' (Linklater 1998*a*: 84). This formulation rightly recognizes the asymmetry of globalization and the non-reciprocal nature of the duties to which it gives rise. Nor is it exactly that 'more dialogue' is incompatible with discharging this duty of 'protection'. My objection is, simply, that more dialogue is by no means the most *obvious* answer to the question of how to discharge it. If harm is being done, then more *justice* rather than more talking is the first requirement. So if we know harm is being, and has been, done, then cosmopolitanism's 'universal communication community' is de trop at best, and an indulgence at worst. Perhaps too much time has been spent listening to critics of the 'universalising project of the Enlightenment' (Linklater 1998*a*: 103), and not enough to those peoples of the Pacific whose homes are disappearing.

I mentioned earlier that the 'dialogic community' is just one of two types of social bond canvassed by dialogic cosmopolitanism. The other is that of belonging to the 'human community', and this belonging is said to give rise to certain duties: 'there are certain duties which the members of these states owe others by virtue of humanity alone' (Linklater 1998*a*: 78). This duty is then given a specific name: 'Notions of world citizenship usually refer to *compassion* for the rest of humanity' (Linklater 1998*a*: 179; emphasis added). In this context Linklater refers approvingly to Michael Walzer's recognition that we have 'Good Samaritan'-type obligations to non-national strangers: 'Walzer argues that in the course of reaching their decisions members should heed the moral principle of "Good Samaritanism" which extends across national boundaries' (Linklater 1998*a*: 80). Presumably Linklater enlists Walzer in this way because of Walzer's well-known suspicion of the idea of international obligation. So, if even Walzer admits to an element of such obligation, then cosmopolitanism's plan to extend it may not be so daft after all.

But this victory has been won at some cost—specifically, at the cost of confounding moral with political obligation. This simultaneously weakens the 'bindingness' of international obligation, and makes it harder for cosmopolitanism to speak of itself as a project of *citizenship*, which is what it wants to do (cf. Linklater 1998*a*: 179, above). Let me take these two points in turn, and I shall return to the latter one in Chapter 2.

First, the Good Samaritan's tending to the injured man at the side of the road was a charitable act. Jesus describes it, significantly, as 'neighbourly' (*Luke* 10:36). Charity is a notoriously weak basis for obligation—it is easily withdrawn ('terribly sorry, no spare change in my pocket this morning'), and the structure of giving contained within it both cements and reproduces the vulnerability of the recipient. Contrast this with justice. The actual act of compensation or the avoidance of justiciable harm can be halted, of course, but the obligation to do justice remains. Similarly, relations of justice are relations between putative equals. In these senses, justice is preferable to charity, yet charity is all that this type of cosmopolitanism is likely to be able to give us as long as belonging to 'the human community' (towards which we can indeed only have supererogatory, Samaritan, obligations) remains the source of the social bond.

Second, if citizenship is to have any meaning at all, then the condition of being a citizen must be distinguishable from being a human being. In other words, there must be a difference between the community of citizens and the community of humanity. Linklater's cosmopolitanism effectively elides these two communities by making the 'Samaritan' source of obligation common to them both. I want to argue that, while this kind of obligation is appropriate for relations between human beings *qua* human beings, it is not appropriately predicated of relations between citizens. Unfortunately, Samaritan obligation is presented by Linklater as apparently the only transnational alternative to other types: '*Inevitably*, a sense of humanitarian obligation has to stand in for shared nationality or common interest in the case of world citizenship' (Linklater 1998*a*: 201; emphasis added), and, 'In circumstances where cultures are otherwise radically different, the commitment to assist the vulnerable rests on *nothing other than* a sense of common humanity' (Linklater 1998*a*: 87; emphasis added).

But one of cosmopolitanism's own tenets offers another option, one which both presents the possibility of more binding and less paternalistic forms of obligation, and enables a distinction between 'citizenship' and 'being human' to be drawn. Linklater writes that 'The main impetus for global moral responsibility arises in the context of increasing transnational harm' (Linklater 1998*a*: 105). Now the relationship between the causers and the victims of harm is completely different from that between the Good Samaritan and the poor unfortunate by the side of the road. The Good Samaritan was not directly or even indirectly responsible for the injured man's plight. In the formulation just quoted, however, Linklater is pointing to *relations of actual harm*. The obligation to compensate for harm, or to take action to avoid it, is not an obligation of charity to be met through the exercise of compassion, but of justice. Justice, as I have pointed out, is a more binding and less paternalistic source and form of obligation than charity, and its political nature takes us out of the realm of 'common humanity' and into the realm of citizenship. This obligation to do justice is a political obligation rather than a more general moral obligation, and is therefore more appropriately predicated of 'being a citizen' than 'being human'.

## Distributive Cosmopolitanism and Beyond

In taking justice to be the principal cosmopolitan concern, what I want to call distributive cosmopolitanism comes closer to the post-cosmopolitan view that I wish to articulate. In a review of the theories and principles of international distributive justice, Simon Caney describes the 'principal cosmopolitan claim' as follows: 'given the reasons we give to defend the distribution of resources and given our convictions about the irrelevance of people's cultural identity to their entitlements, it follows that the scope of justice should be global' (Caney 2001: 977). I do not propose to defend that view here (although see the rest of Caney 2001 for a useful summary of the view and its opponents); I simply record that it forms a part of the post-cosmopolitan picture without completing it. The same might be said of any number of similar-sounding characterizations, such as Charles Jones's: 'The fundamental idea is that each person affected by an institutional arrangement should be given equal consideration' (Jones 1999: 15). I said earlier that distributive cosmopolitanism gives us defensible principles for redistribution, but inadequate reasons for action. In the form of a question, then, having expanded the scope of justice beyond the state, how persuasive are this cosmopolitanism's reasons for actually doing justice? The source of obligation for distributive cosmopolitanism is a theory of 'moral personality' according to which 'people's entitlements are independent of their culture, race and nationality' (Caney 2001: 979). The corollary of this is that there is something about all people—their autonomy or their possession of rights, for example—that entitles them to an in principle equal share of whatever is being distributed. This is a step beyond dialogic cosmopolitanism in two senses. First, it entails a specifically political type of obligation as opposed to a more broadly moral type, and this opens the door to a potentially more convincing conception of citizenship beyond the state. Second, it deals in the currency of justice rather than compassion, and the obligations connected with the former are less revocable than those related to the latter.

What is common to both dialogic and distributive cosmopolitanism, though, is a thin and non-material account of the ties that bind members of the cosmopolitan community together. For the former it is 'common humanity', expressed through the 'ethical commitment to open dialogue'. For the latter it is again 'common humanity', but expressed this time through the undifferentiated possession of certain characteristics that entitle their possessors to just treatment. Post-cosmopolitanism, in contrast, offers a thickly material account of the ties that bind, created not by mental activity, but by the material production and reproduction of daily life in an unequal and asymmetrically globalizing world. In this conception, the political space of obligation is not fixed as taking the form of the state, or the nation, or the European Union, or the globe, but is rather 'produced' by the activities of individuals and groups with the capacity to spread and impose themselves in geographical, diachronic, and—especially important in the context of this book—ecological space.

My most general point, then, is that globalization is best regarded as a producer of this political space of asymmetrical obligation. Another way of putting this is to say that globalization consistently turns relationships that we might have thought to be 'Samaritan' into relationships of citizenship, in the sense I referred to above in my discussion of Linklater. Judith Lichtenberg, to whom I shall have cause to refer again in Chapter 2, has described this phenomenon as follows: 'My claim is that history has involved the gradual (or perhaps not so gradual) transformation of the earth from a collection of many relatively open worlds to one closed one' (Lichtenberg 1981: 86). This is especially evident in the environmental context:

Some of the relationships in virtue of which the earth now constitutes one world are so pervasive and far-reaching that they are difficult to pinpoint or to measure. There are also actions that may have harmful consequences without any direct involvement between agents and those affected. For these reasons it is easy to ignore them as sources of obligation. (Lichtenberg 1981: 87).

And it is not only the source of the obligation that is in question here, but its nature, too. Take the issue of 'natural' disasters, for example. If a volcano erupts, we can be fairly sure that the disaster is indeed a natural one, in the sense of having no anthropogenic origin. But can we be confident that the increasing incidence of massive floods around the world can be similarly described? A majority of climate scientists suggest that, although the disaggregated impacts of global warming are very hard to predict, we are likely to experience an increased incidence of extreme weather events—so called 'strange weather'. So when floods devastate large areas of developing countries, we congratulate ourselves for the generous quantities of aid we offer to alleviate the suffering. From the 'closed earth' point of view, though, the campaigning issue is not so much about how generous aid should be, but whether 'aid' is the appropriate category at all. If global warming is principally caused by wealthy countries, and if global warming is at least a part cause of strange weather, then monies should be transferred as a matter of compensatory justice rather than as aid or charity.

Globalization, properly understood, then, changes the source and nature of obligation, and renders 'thin' cosmopolitanism's account both of the nature of the transnational community and of the obligations at work in it inadequate to the task of remedying globalization's special harms. So the link between my critique of Held-type globalization and thin cosmopolitanism is as follows. Held fails to make the asymmetrical nature of globalization sufficiently central to his analysis. Thin cosmopolitanism is similarly constructed in and around an undifferentiated 'common humanity', and the obligations to which membership of the human community gives rise. Recognizing the asymmetrical nature of globalization, on the other hand, simultaneously makes for a more accurate picture of the processes of globalization itself, and also provides the resources for a more robust account of transnational 'community' and of the obligations contained within it. This is not a cosmopolitan community at all, but a post-cosmopolitan relationship of actual harm, made possible by globalization and illustrated by some of the

74915

processes at work in it. In the hope that I have adequately sketched what I regard as the key features of globalization and post-cosmopolitanism, I can now move on to consider the more specific context within which ecological citizenship (Chapter 3) is inscribed—the context of citizenship itself.

# Chapter 2

# Three Types of Citizenship

Two types of citizenship, most commonly called 'liberal' and 'civic republican', dominate the intellectual and political landscape. My contention is that changes of sufficient structural and ideological gravity are taking place in the world today for it to be appropriate to canvass the emergence of a third type of citizenship, which I shall call 'post-cosmopolitan'. I am not seeking to replace liberal and civic republican citizenship with post-cosmopolitanism, but merely to argue that the conditions in which we find ourselves 'demand' this new and additional articulation. The structural change is globalization, one of the subjects of Chapter 1. This phenomenon obliges us to rethink the spatial frameworks of citizenship, in particular. Can we make sense of citizenship beyond the state? I shall argue that we can, and that there is an alternative to doing so in the currently popular cosmopolitan fashion. The ideological influence is feminism. Feminist analyses of citizenship have led

to reconsiderations of virtue, of the reassertion of citizen–
citizen relations as well as citizen–state relations, and of the
sources and nature of citizenship obligations. Together, themes
in globalization and feminism point towards a third citizenship
that cannot be politically or discursively contained in either
liberal or civic republican forms. While globalization and feminism provide the context for post-cosmopolitan citizenship,
there is a phenomenon that gives rise to its most precise
articulation—environmental politics. In Chapter 3, I shall try to
show that environmental politics can be articulated in terms of
citizenship, and that the nature of this politics 'demands' that
the articulation be of a post-cosmopolitan variety.

## *Method*

Most discussions of citizenship exhibit two kinds of shortcoming. First, while citizenship as an idea and as a practice is clearly
multidimensional, many approaches to it focus on only one
or two of them, thereby offering a distorted and incomplete
picture. A typical instance of this is the oft-drawn contrast
between the idea of citizenship as rights-claiming or as the
exercise of responsibilities. This distinction is indeed an important one, but it is not exhaustive of the conceptual map that
makes up citizenship. Part of the intention of what follows
here is therefore to sketch the map that will inform the rest of
this book.

The second problem is that, even where approaches are more
comprehensive, the conceptual packages deployed are often
static rather than dynamic, and those who use them are sometimes reluctant to entertain the idea that changing conditions
(both 'real' and 'conceptual') can imply changing reference
points for citizenship itself. Just as, for example, the secular
patriot of the twelfth and thirteenth centuries in Italy would
have found it hard to conceive of citizenship in terms of

the modern rights-claimant of the contemporary nation-state (Reisenberg 1992: 118), so we find it hard to entertain the idea now that citizenship can have meaning outside the nation-state—that cosmopolitan citizenship, for example, makes sense *as citizenship*. We need, therefore, to take seriously Gershon Shafir's warning that 'the historical record indicates that when social conditions change, some aspects of the themes of citizenship change with them' (1998: 4).

This view is endorsed by Peter Reisenberg (1992) in his exhaustive survey of the development of the idea. 'One premise of this book', he writes, 'is that there have been two citizenships, forms of institution different enough from each other to justify such a classification and interpretation. The first lasted from the time of the Greek city-state until French Revolution; the second has been in existence since then' (1992: p. xviii). 'Today', he says, 'men and women of at least the West live under the second citizenship, the result of some of the great forces of modern history' (1992: p. xix). Among these 'great forces', Reisenberg registers the change in the scale of public life, from a face-to-face environment in which people 'knew and knew of each other' (1992: p. xix) to larger forms of social organization where most political relationships were anonymous. He also points out that 'from the late Middle Ages on, there took place a progressive and meaningful assimilation of the "citizen" into the "subject", the transformation of the active political person into the passive political person' (Reisenberg 1992: p. xx). Both of these observations square with the evolution of republican forms of citizenship into what we now regard as the liberal form of citizenship, in which rights-claiming comes to take precedence over civic virtue. The key point is that Greek, Roman, Spartan, and medieval citizens would not have recognized the 'second' citizenship to which Reisenberg refers, and so it is essential to deploy a historical sensibility when considering the shape—and particularly the future shape—of citizenship.

## Three Types of Citizenship

I can most easily illustrate the issues at stake by analysing Bryan Turner's representative 1990 article, 'A Theory of Citizenship'. Turner refers to 'two crucial variables' in citizenship theory. 'The first', he writes, 'concerns the passive or active nature of citizenship, depending on whether citizenship is developed from above (via the state) or from below (in terms of more participatory institutions, such as trade unions)' (1990: 189). 'The second', he continues, 'is the relationship between the public and the private arenas within civil society. A conservative view of citizenship (as passive and private) contrasts with a more revolutionary idea of active and public citizenship' (1990: 189). Turner concludes his examination with this claim: 'By combining these two dimensions, it is possible to produce a historically dynamic theory of four types of democratic polities as societal contexts for the realisation of citizenship rights' (1990: 189).

Turner's intention here is to draw up a comprehensive list of the dimensions around which citizenship-talk is organized, and there is no doubt that the ones he comes up with are of crucial importance. 'Active citizenship', for example, is recognized as a distinctive type of citizenship, and the contrast between the public and private arenas brings into relief the *agora*-orientated inspiration of much citizenship theory and practice. The claim to comprehensiveness is further enhanced by the combinative move made by Turner, whereby two contrasts produce four 'types' of citizenship context.

But this claim is undermined by only having two contrasts in the first place; more aspects of citizenship need to be taken into account. Turner does not mention, for example, the idea of citizenship virtue—a notion that may not be present in most contemporary understandings of citizenship, but which has most certainly been a feature of historical citizenship experience. The addition of virtue- and non-virtue-based conceptions of citizenship would have offered Turner a third contrast, providing nine possible types of citizenship context.

He makes no reference, either, to considerations of territoriality, most probably because dominant contemporary forms of citizenship take territoriality for granted. This is to say that citizenship is understood in terms of membership of a territory whose shape and size is determined according to the rules of state sovereignty. But a truly 'historically dynamic theory' would recognize that not all conceptions of citizenship *have* taken these constraints for granted, and that Alexandrine and Kantian notions of citizenship, for example, and their more recent manifestations in the guise of cosmopolitan citizenship, have been explicitly non-territorial. We now have four contrasts, and therefore sixteen combinations of citizenship context.

And there is one final distinction to which we should draw attention—implicit rather than explicit in Turner's typology, but extremely important nonetheless, and referred to briefly above. Turner refers to 'the realisation of citizenship rights' in a way that might lead us to suspect that rights-claiming is the citizen's centre of gravity. Once again, though, this is a contemporary snapshot of the content of citizenship, rather than the 'historically dynamic' theory that Turner is aiming for. A broader historical perspective would reveal that the exercise of obligation, or responsibility, has been a crucial element in some conceptions of citizenship, and that the 'dynamic' of citizenship has often been, precisely, that of a contest between rights- and obligation-based notions of it.

This commentary on Turner should make it clear that the domain of citizenship, as a concept, is much broader than his 'theory of citizenship' would have us believe. As a minimum we should think in terms of four contrasts: rights and obligations; territorial and non-territorial conceptions of citizenship; the public and the private arenas as possible sites of citizenship activity; and competing virtue- and non-virtue-based ideas of citizenship. This fuller set of contrasts will enable us to appreciate better the nature of debates in contemporary citizenship in general, and to assess the challenge represented by 'ecological citizenship', in particular. This will be the theme of Chapter 3.

None of these contrasts exists in isolation from the others, of course, and full conceptions of citizenship are usually made up of specific combinations of them. As I pointed out at the beginning of this chapter, it is very common in this context to organize discussions of citizenship around two broad types: civic republican and liberal. Derek Heater's view is representative: 'it is most helpful to easy comprehension—not to mention quite fashionable—to distinguish between two traditions and interpretations of the nature of citizenship. These are the civic republican style, which places its stress on duties, and the liberal style, which places its stress on rights' (1999: 4). (Note Heater's committing of what we might call the 'one contrast fallacy', discussed above in connection with Turner. Heater would have us believe that the contrast between liberal and civic republican citizenship can be explained solely in terms of the rights/duties distinction. I hope I have said enough already to indicate that these two types of citizenship are likely to be much richer in content than this single contrast would suggest.)

Indeed at this point the shortcomings of the one- or two-contrast approach to citizenship analysis are very apparent. The supposedly sharp distinction between liberal and civic republican citizenship is bought at the cost of defining them *only* in terms of the rights/duties or individual/communitarian distinctions. If, however, we add in the other distinctions discussed above, these two apparently very different types of citizenship turn out to have rather a lot in common. This is important not only in analytical terms, but also with a view to grasping the full extent of the political implications of contemporary challenges to traditional conceptions of citizenship. Heater implies that there is nothing 'outside' the liberal and civic republican categories of citizenship, but the multidimensional approach to citizenship that I am proposing shows that there is indeed an

**Table 2.1  Three types of citizenship**

| First: liberal | Second: civic republican | Third: post-cosmopolitan |
|---|---|---|
| Rights/entitlements (contractual) | Duties/responsibilities (contractual) | Duties/responsibilities (non-contractual) |
| Public sphere | Public sphere | Public and private spheres |
| Virtue-free | 'Masculine' virtue | 'Feminine' virtue |
| Territorial (discriminatory) | Territorial (discriminatory) | Non-territorial (non-discriminatory) |

alternative third citizenship—both logically and in actual political fact.

It may help to have the three citizenships laid out in a table, with the key one- or two-word descriptors in each of them awaiting explication in what follows (Table 2.1). These three citizenships are not as hermetically distinct as the tabular form might suggest. The descriptors serve simply to highlight what is most different in each case, and this does not preclude a certain amount of sharing of characteristics. Let me also stress that these are characterizations of evidently complex and contested terms; I hope that they will be read in the appropriate illustrative and contrastive spirit.

Although not formally included in my list of contrasts, I should mention the often-made distinction between active and passive citizenship. From an analytical point of view this distinction has much to commend it at first sight, particularly if it is placed alongside the contrast between rights and duties. From this perspective, active citizenship has to do with the discharging of duties and responsibilities to the political community and its members, while passive citizenship is associated with sitting back and claiming the rights that are due to the individual qua citizen. The distinction between activity and passivity begins to unravel, though, with the recognition that it is tendentious to regard a 'preoccupation with formal rights' as a purely passive business. British ex-Prime Minister John Major's idea of the 'Citizen's Charter' was much derided at the time it was developed. Rooted as it was, and is, in the New Right conception of citizens' rights—the right to have services delivered economically and efficiently—it appeared to have little to do with the kinds of social entitlements that had come to be synonymous with citizenship. But a moment's reflection leads us to see that the 'citizen as consumer' is in fact a very active individual, comparing prices, demanding satisfaction from public services, and chasing up failures of service delivery when they occur. I do not propose here, though, to include the active/passive distinction in the discussion that follows since it is so closely bound up with the issue of sites of citizenship activity that I shall be considering in detail. This brief survey has shown, though, that once again a contrast generally thought to be central to the distinction between liberal and civic republican citizenship is not as secure it appears. Let me pursue this now through a detailed examination of the contrasts outlined in Table 2.1.

## Rights and Responsibilities—and Contracts

I have indicated that this contrast is indeed one area in which liberal and civic republican citizenships differ, and this is reflected in Table 2.1. I shall argue, though, that the contrast hides an underlying similarity. This is that both liberal and civic republican citizenship subscribe to a contractual view of the relationship between the citizen and the state. Post-cosmopolitanism, on the other hand, eschews the language and implied reciprocity of contract.

It is worth pointing up both the centrality of the contrast between rights and responsibilities in citizenship theory, and the dominance of rights in the partnership: 'the view of citizenship that is implicit in much postwar political theory...is defined almost entirely in terms of the possession of rights' (Kymlicka and Norman 1994: 354; see also Roche 1992: 20). In intellectual terms, the reason for this is not hard to find— T. H. Marshall. Nearly all contemporary accounts of modern citizenship begin with Marshall's *Citizenship and Social Class and other Essays* (1950), a collection which contains his essay of the same name, originally given as the Alfred Marshall lecture in Cambridge in 1949. In that essay, Marshall offers his famous account of the development of citizenship, beginning with the winning of civil rights (liberty of the person, freedom of speech, and so on), moving through political rights (the right to participate in the exercise of political power), and ending with social rights (the right to a degree of social and economic security). The influence of this typology has been immense, to the point where it is sometimes hard to conceive of citizenship in terms other than those of rights and entitlement. Ralf Dahrendorf, for example, says that modern politics is about two great themes: *provisions* (i.e. goods), and access to them, or *entitlements*. For him, 'citizenship belongs squarely on the entitlement side of this picture' (Dahrendorf 1994: 12), and this is a belief apparently shared by many others.

This is not the place for an extended commentary on Marshall's work (for that, see Bulmer and Rees 1996)—I simply want to highlight its authoritative status, and to argue in favour of a broader historical and theoretical canvas in our attempt to map citizenship more comprehensively. Indeed, in Britain at least, one does not need to go back much further than a few decades to find a completely different *Zeitgeist* as far as characterizations of citizenship are concerned. In a series of lectures on 'Constructive Citizenship' given at Glasgow University in 1926–7, L. P. Jacks made what now looks to be the startling claim that *'man is by nature a responsible being'* (n.d.: 210; emphasis in the original), and it therefore follows, he says, that, '[T]he *right to responsibility* is the outstanding right of the citizen. In the absence of it all other "rights" amount to nothing.

His rights and his duties coalesce at that point. He has duties, yes, but the *right to duty* underlies them all' (n.d.: 210–1). This formulation takes the language of rights and enlists it to make a point that would have been instantly recognizable to his contemporary audience, but which looks distinctly odd to us today.

What emerges from a broader historical and cultural perspective than that found in Marshall's overwhelmingly influential rights-based typology, is a battle between rights and duties for the status of citizenship's defining characteristic. It is important for me to establish this since the 'post-cosmopolitan citizenship' I am developing here is characterized by a focus on duty and responsibility, rather than on rights. It should be said that citizenship duties do receive some attention in Marshall's seminal work—duties for the employed to make compulsory contributions, to look for work, to use the strike weapon sparingly, and so on—but they are understated. Recently the focus on citizen duties and responsibilities has become more explicit and a number of commentators have talked of the 'need to supplement (or replace) the passive acceptance of citizenship rights with the active exercise of citizenship responsibilities and virtues, including economic self-reliance, political participation, and even civility' (Kymlicka and Norman 1994: 355), and the way in which '[T]he welfare state can be argued to have appeared to promote a rights-based and relatively duty-free and unreciprocal conception of citizenship' (Roche 1992: 31; see also Rees 1995: 316).

The emphasis on social duty and responsibility has increasingly been stressed by governments of the centre-left, and those centre-left governments that have picked up where radical right-wing reforming governments left off—such as Britain's Prime Minister Tony Blair's 'New Labour'—have been particularly keen on this trend. Geoff Mulgan, for example, writes of a general 'unease that the left's ideas about citizenship should end up as nothing more than a package of rights without obligations, a programme for a loose society in which relationships are contingent and undemanding' (Mulgan 1991: 41). Anthony Giddens, too, widely regarded as Tony Blair's favourite intellectual, has homed in on the rights/responsibilities theme as the key defining feature of the famed 'Third Way': '[O]ne might suggest as a prime motto for the new politics, *no rights without responsibilities*. Government has a whole cluster of responsibilities for its citizens and others, including the protection of the vulnerable. Old-style social democracy, however, was inclined to treat rights as unconditional claims' (Giddens 1998: 65; emphasis in the original).

In sum, as Mulgan sagely and aphoristically puts it: 'Utopias maximise freedom. They never maximise responsibilities' (Mulgan 1991: 42). A defining feature of the post-cosmopolitan citizenship towards which I am working here is that it swims against the tide in this respect. This citizenship is part of the palpable shift taking place in the Western world regarding the 'remoralization' of politics. Fundamentally, this remoralization has to do with the rehabilitation of virtue in the language and practice of politics. Will Kymlicka and Wayne Norman have pointed out that one of the reasons for the recent revival of citizenship as an idea is the growing awareness that the unadulterated pursuit of self-interest undercuts the kinds of conditions that make a reasonable pursuit of self-interest possible, and that some commitment to the intersubjectivity of social life is desirable: 'the health and stability of a modern democracy depends, not only on the justice of its "basic structure" but also on the qualities and attitudes of its citizens' (Kymlicka and Norman 1994: 352). Similarly, Maurice Roche (1992: 242) has commented that:

[T]he politics of citizenship has for generations formulated its goals, fought its battles and found its voice in the discourse of rights. In the late twentieth century it also needs to be able to speak, to act and to understand itself in the language of citizens' personal responsibility and social obligation, in the discourse of duties as well as of rights. (Roche 1992: 242)

It is this focus on duty and virtue that distinguishes, in part, my putative 'post-cosmopolitan citizenship'.

But while this might distinguish such citizenship from the liberal and rights-based type, is not duty also a feature of civic republican citizenship? And if so, how do civic republican and post-cosmopolitan citizenship differ from one another? Earlier I made the point that although liberal and civic republican citizenships do indeed differ in terms of their respective stress on the rights and duties of citizenship, these differences are underpinned by an explicitly *contractual* basis for these rights and duties. In this respect, both types of citizenship share common ideological foundations—foundations undermined in and by post-cosmopolitan citizenship.

The contractual idiom is explicit in the contemporary revival of citizenship. We have seen Anthony Giddens referring to 'no rights without responsibilities', a formula which has individuals claiming rights which will only be redeemed if they discharge their citizen responsibilities effectively. On this view, citizenship is regarded as a contract between the citizen and the state, in which the citizen claims rights against the state, but according to which the citizen also undertakes to contribute to the state's ends by paying taxes, for example, and by seeking work when unemployed. This is a reciprocity in which rights are earned.

The contractual view of citizenship is very common—so common, indeed, that it is rarely explicitly articulated, let alone explicitly defended. Maurice Roche, for example, suggests, as we have seen, that '[T]he welfare state can be argued to have appeared to promote a rights-based and relatively duty-free and unreciprocal conception of citizenship' (Roche 1992: 31). I agree with the broad sentiment of this, but what is interesting for our present purpose is Roche's implicit subscribing to a *reciprocal* understanding of the relationship between citizen rights and obligations: the citizen has rights in respect of the state, but these rights entail reciprocal obligations. Roche underpins this with what he calls a 'common sense notion of morality' (1992: 31) involving the 'interactional reciprocity between people involved in moral action' (Roche 1992: 31; see also Stewart 1995: 71). The enlisting of 'common sense' notions of anything should set alarm bells ringing, and this is especially true of common sense notions of morality—as I shall explain below.

Similarly, Richard Dagger's provocative attempt to make civic service compatible with liberal freedom (i.e. to bring together two major themes in liberal and civic republican citizenship) is informed by the unremarked assumption that such service is the entry fee to the palace of entitlements that the modern liberal state has to offer: 'the point of the service is not to earn a wage or to turn a profit but to do one's duty—to do something for the other members of the community *in return for* the protection of the law and the other benefits of membership that one has received and hopes to continue to receive' (2000: 3; emphasis added).

The contractual view runs very deep, as in Michael Ignatieff's discussion of what he calls the 'myth of citizenship'. He consistently views citizenship as a bargain between the individual citizen and the political community, and he argues that if citizenship is under strain, that is because the bargain is a bad one—by which he means that the individual citizen is not getting enough out of the bargain. The nodal point of Ignatieff's argument is taxation, and he locates the onset of the 'crisis of citizenship' at the point where '[P]eople begin to ask why they are paying more for declining levels of public service' (Ignatieff 1995: 69–70). In contrast with this, post-cosmopolitan citizenship is explicitly non-contractual and has nothing to do with bargains between citizens and the political community.

It might be argued at this point, though, that citizenship is *definitionally* contractual. On this view, citizenship relations are those between the individual and the state, and both historical experience and normative theory confirm that these relations are—and should be—best described by the contractual idiom. There is certainly something to be said for this view; indeed, if there were not, then my claim that both liberal and civic republican notions of citizenship have contractualism in common would not make much sense. As John Horton has put it: 'The reason why reciprocal/contractual models of citizenship are attractive is precisely because they try to explain how the rights (and duties) of citizenship are circumscribed to citizens. The point about citizenship relations is that they only hold between citizens, and not, for example, between parents and children or peoples of one state and another' (1998, personal communication). This is a powerful point, but it forgets that it too is working with an explicit 'model' of human relationships drawn from outside citizenship theory. It is not clear why 'reciprocal/contractual' models of relationships should be any more definitive of citizenship than friendship models, for example. 'Contract' is not, as Horton seems to suggest, a form of relationship specific to citizenship at all. If it is specific to any area of social life, it is the sphere of trade and exchange (although this does not mean that it is appropriate to that sphere alone, and I am not at all saying that it is wholly inappropriate to citizenship). To this extent, the language of contract does not mark off citizenship as a special and distinct kind of relationship but, rather, associates it closely with the juridical–economic sphere and the expectations and assumptions that lie therein. Contract is therefore as much an ideological as a definitional feature of citizenship. Once this is recognized, other ways of articulating citizenship relations become possible.

The historical record supports this alternative view. Patricia Harris writes, for example, that 'contractual relations have come to substitute for the common bonds of reciprocity and mutuality which shaped social citizenship in the earlier part of the twentieth century' (1999: 46). Here Harris is calling into question the motivational source of reciprocity. In the contractual idiom, the ultimate source is the penalty imposed if the contract is broken. This threat of sanction is quite explicit in Giddens' 'no rights without responsibilities' formulation, and it lies at the heart of the 'workfare' programme that is so central to Third Way social policy. Harris, on the other hand, points to the motivation of 'mutuality', according to which reciprocity is built into the normative understanding of the relationship itself rather than driven by external threat of sanction. From the 'mutual' point of view, it would be unthinkable to act in anything other than the appropriately reciprocal manner.

Yet, although Harris might tempt us to move away from contract, she is still living in the land of reciprocity. There are, of course, other forms of human relationship that are not only non-contractual but non-reciprocal too. As Nancy Fraser and Linda Gordon have pointed out: 'American thinking about social provision has been shaped largely by images drawn from civil citizenship, especially images of contract. The result is a cultural tendency to focus on two, rather extreme, forms of human relationship: discrete contractual exchanges of equivalents, on the one hand, and unreciprocated, unilateral charity, on the other' (Fraser and Gordon 1994: 91). I want to suggest the possibility of *unreciprocated and unilateral* citizenship obligations, and to claim that this type of obligation is both definitive of 'post-cosmopolitan citizenship', as well as that which distinguishes it most obviously from liberal citizenship *and* from the reciprocity of civic republican citizenship.

Critics are of course right that we must distinguish between the obligations of citizenship and broader 'humanitarian' obligations. We must, if you will, distinguish between the Good Samaritan and the Good Citizen, or between the obligations that it would be benevolent to fulfil and those that it would be wrong not to fulfil. This argument normally takes place on the terrain of the nature of obligations themselves. So it will be argued that care and compassion, for example, are not citizenship virtues, while the disposition to seek a balance between private and public interest is. But this is only one aspect of an analytics of obligation. We need to take into account not only the nature of obligations (obligation to do what?), but also their source (why are we obliged?), and their object (to whom or to what are obligations owed?). Following this, I want to suggest that it is the *source* of obligation, rather than what the obligation might actually be, that distinguishes citizenship from a broader humanitarianism.

Attempting to articulate a cosmopolitan view of international morality, Judith Lichtenberg (to whom I referred in Chapter 1) distinguishes between what she calls 'historical' and 'moral' arguments. The moral view has it that 'A owes something positive to B . . . not in virtue of any causal role he has had in B's situation or any prior relationship or agreement, but just because, for example, he is able to benefit B or alleviate his plight' (Lichtenberg 1981: 80). In contrast, the historical view suggests that 'what A owes to B he owes in virtue of some antecedent action, undertaking, agreement, relationship, or the like' (Lichtenberg 1981: 81). The moral view is exactly that adopted by the Good Samaritan, or by the purveyor of charity, and we should not view this as a source of citizenship obligation. The historical view, though, offers a 'materialist' account of a more binding type of reason for obligation. This view contains 'contract' as one kind of reason, but is not exhausted by it. Note that an 'antecedent action' as well an 'agreement' is enough to trigger this kind of obligation. Note also that adopting this 'source' position leaves open the *nature* of citizenship obligations. We should not jump too hastily to the conclusion that care and compassion cannot be citizenship virtues, since what counts is only that there be some broadly 'historical' source of obligation. I shall come back to this in the section on 'Citizenship virtues'. Most crucially, neither reciprocation nor bilateralism is a necessary feature of historical forms of obligation. It is entirely possible to think of antecedent actions that will call forth unilateral obligations—compensatory justice has this kind of structure, for example.

Earlier we saw Peter Reisenberg remarking that a change in the scale of public life was one of the factors that led from what he calls 'first' to 'second' citizenship. A similarly seismic change is taking place today in the guise of globalization. From our point of view, as I suggested in Chapter 1, the critical feature of globalization is the structure of obligation that comes with it. The networks of effect that are at work in globalization amount to precisely the 'antecedent actions' that prompt Lichtenberg-type obligations. Moreover this is not reciprocity but a version of the asymmetrical interdependence thesis—the recognition that the actions of some affect the life chances of distant strangers. The one modification I would make to the Lichtenberg picture is that to call these obligations 'historical' in her sense is to misrepresent their nature in a globalized world. Recall that for Lichtenberg the historical view has it that 'what A owes to B he owes in virtue of some antecedent action, undertaking, agreement, relationship, or the like'. In a globalizing world the notion of 'antecedence' wears thin, as both space *and* time tend towards collapse. Thus, in postmodern parlance, inhabitants of globalizing nations are *always already* acting on others, as when—to return to the example offered in Chapter 1—our use of fossil fuels causes the release of gases that contribute to global warming. It is this recognition that calls forth the virtues and practices of citizenship. Note once again that the distinction between the Good Samaritan and the Good Citizen is preserved. The obligations associated with the former are those that it would be simply desirable to fulfil, in some broadly virtuous, benevolent, and supererogatory sense; those of the latter are obligations that it would be wrong not to fulfil.

While this is a citizenship with international and intergenerational dimensions, its responsibilities are asymmetrical.

Its obligations fall on those, precisely, with the capacity to 'always already' act on others. This follows from Vandana Shiva's insight, referred to in Chapter 1, that, 'the construction of the global environment narrows the South's options while increasing the North's. Through its global reach, the North exists in the South, but the South exists only within itself, since it has no global reach. Thus the South can *only* exist locally, while only the North exists globally' (Shiva 1998: 233). This implies that post-cosmopolitan citizenship responsibilities are for those in the North—or, more precisely, for those in the North implicated in 'narrowing the South's options'. In the most general terms, globalization gives rise to structural relations that suggest the possibility of political obligations of a non-reciprocal and unilateral type. I shall say more on the specifically environmental aspects of this in Chapter 3.

To summarize, we saw in Table 2.1 that the distinction between rights and obligations is a key way of separating liberal from civic republican conceptions of citizenship. However, I have shown that these apparently different conceptions share a common expectation of reciprocity between the citizen and the political community, and that the dominant modern understanding of such reciprocity is underpinned by an ideological commitment to contract. I hope to have shown how contract has a contingent rather than a necessary connection with citizenship, and that it is based upon a social ontology of autonomous individuals freely entering relations of trade and exchange. An alternative social ontology of material embeddedness calls into question the 'common sense' reciprocal expectations of morality to be found in the contractual idiom, and opens up the possibility of alternative models of citizenship relations. This debate about the source and nature of 'third citizenship' obligations is in fact closely related to the issue of virtue, and I will take the opportunity to say more about it later in the chapter.

## *Public and Private*

Citizenship has almost always been associated with what has come to be known as 'the public sphere'. As Pocock remarks, Aristotle's dictum, that 'man is a political animal', 'depends upon a rigorous separation of public from private, or *polis* from *oikos*' (1995: 32). Aristotle also judged the public to be more worthy than the private: 'he did insist specifically that the realm of *oeconomia*—the household realm in which the material necessities of daily life were reproduced—was a lesser realm than the public' (Ignatieff 1995: 56). In citizenship theory this separation has been handed down virtually intact, to the point where the much-commented recent revival of citizenship has revolved almost entirely around the 'rehabilitation of elements of what could be called in shorthand form the "classical civic tradition"... the conception of citizenship stemming from Aristotle which sees the citizen first and foremost as an active participant in the public affairs of the *polis*' (Burchell 1995: 540, and see Walzer 1989: 211).

The identification of citizenship with the public arena, combined with the idea of citizenship as a privileged and discriminatory status, serves neatly to reinforce the subordinate status of what goes on in the private sphere of human activity. There are a number of ways in which this might be expressed, but the distinction between spheres of 'freedom' and 'necessity' is particularly striking:

In the context of the Greek city-state, the *polis*, citizenship appeared as a double process of emancipation.... it was the transcendence of the instrumental sphere of necessity, in which we toil to satisfy our material wants, into the sphere of freedom.... This contrast has been conceptualised in multiple forms—for example, as emancipation from the private sphere of the household (*oikos*) into the public sphere of political life (*polis*).                        (Shafir 1998: 3)

I shall pick up the theme of a 'citizenship of the sphere of necessity' in Chapter 3, but for now we again see that the distinction between the public and the private in the context of citizenship is *political and ideological* at least as much as it is analytical. Feminist commentaries on citizenship have identified a

male bias in the tradition of citizenship—found in the dichotomy between the private household (*oikos*) and the public sphere (*polis*)—that was central to the citizenship tradition from its inception in ancient Greece. The consequent portrayal of the *public sphere* as transcendent, rational, and ultimately masculine and of the *private sphere* as the feminine realm of emotions and the weak body has not disappeared.

(Shafir 1998: 21)

This presents feminists, and anyone else for whom the private sphere is a bona fide site of political activity, with a problem as far as citizenship is concerned. For if citizenship is definitionally an activity carried out in the public arena, then a politics of the private arena cannot be a politics of citizenship. John Pocock neatly summarizes the options:

If one wants to make citizenship available to those to whom it has been denied on the grounds that they are too much involved in the world of things—in material, productive, domestic, or reproductive relationships—one has to choose between emancipating them from those relationships and denying that these relationships are negative components in the definition of citizenship. If one chooses the latter course, one is in search of a new definition of citizenship, differing radically from the definition articulated by Aristotle, a definition in which public and private are not rigorously separated and the barriers between them have become permeable or have disappeared altogether. In the latter case, one will have to decide whether the concept of the 'public' has survived at all, whether it has merely become contingent or incidental, or has actually been denied any distinctive meaning. And if that is what has happened, the concept of citizenship may have disappeared as well. (Pocock 1995: 33)

Ruth Lister glosses this with a specific example: '[I]n the political arena, is the objective to challenge the conditions, including the sexual division of labour, which curtail women's rights as citizens or to develop concepts and practices of citizenship which take into account the sexual division of labour and women's caring role within it?' (1991: 70). Similarly, she asks, 'In the social arena, is the aim to change the nature of social citizenship rights so that earning is no longer privileged over caring in the allocation of those rights or is it to improve women's access to the labour market so that they can compete on equal terms with men and gain the same employment-linked social citizenship rights?' (1991: 70).

One of the reasons why feminists have this debate at all is because many of them regard citizenship as a prize worth capturing. The idea is that citizenship, for better or worse, has acquired a discursive progressive authority that it would be foolish to discard in the attempt to create wholly new languages in which to express feminist aspirations. However, the 'subversion or deconstruction' of which Pocock (1995: 31) speaks presents its own problems, since there may come a moment at which the deconstructive animus lays such waste to citizenship that what remains is unrecognizable *as* citizenship. At this point the original reason for enlisting citizenship to political service—its discursive authority—is self-evidently lost.

My own view is that this reaction refuses to take seriously the central feminist point regarding the need, precisely, to politicize the private sphere—to recognize, in other words, that the private sphere is a site of the exercise of power. Once this step is taken, the possibility of linking citizenship (which is, indeed, a *political* concept) with the private sphere, is opened up. This, as I understand it, is Raia Prokhovnik's point when she writes that, 'it is *not* that women need to be liberated from the *private* realm, in order to take part in the public realm as equal citizens, but that women—and men—already undertake responsibilities of citizenship in both the public and the private realms' (1998: 84). Prokhovnik's point is that many practices that we would not normally regard as citizenship practices should indeed be so regarded; that, for example, 'the "natural obligations" parents are seen to have in bringing up children should also be recognized and valued as ethically-grounded "civic obligations", as part of citizenship' (1998: 88). This, in sum, 'allows for activity within the "private" realm to be recognized as also constituting a legitimate form of activity of citizens' (Prokhovnik 1998: 97). This is not to politicize the whole of the private sphere in an invasive way, but to recognize that some of the things we do in the private sphere have citizenly characteristics.

In Pocock's terms, then, our 'third' citizenship seems to entail a 'new definition' of citizenship, one in which the public–private distinction is modulated. This is not a blurring of the distinction between public and private, but a redrawing of the lines according to which the distinction is made. In part this is due to the recognition, neatly captured by Paul Clarke, of the possibility of *private* actions having virtuous *public* implications. In connection with what he calls 'deep citizenship', he writes that '[W]hat makes it an action of civic virtue is the degree to which, while being possibly private in origin and particular in concern, it nevertheless sets selfishness, sectarianism and sectionalism aside in favour of acting into the universal' (Clarke 1996: 117). This is one way of understanding Pnina Werbner's observation of 'the fluidity of the private/public divide as a constantly shifting and contested demarcation' (1999: 227). Given this fluidity, it is a mistake to erect untranscendable distinctions between public and private acts and better to realize that some of the latter can be regarded as acts of citizenship, properly speaking. Prokhovnik writes, again, that, 'many feminists would argue that the desire of many women to take with them their experiences as mothers and carers *into* the public realm is valid and enriching for the public realm' (1998: 91).

Far from being a lesser realm than the public, then, the private sphere may be a crucial site of citizenship activity. 'Consider the many ways that public policy relies on responsible personal lifestyle decisions', write Will Kymlicka and Wayne Norman, 'the state cannot protect the environment if citizens are unwilling to reduce, reuse, and recycle in their own homes' (Kymlicka and Norman 1994: 360). Our 'third citizenship' is therefore immersed in Pocock's 'world of things', the world of necessity, and resists Ruth Lister's claim that the private realm is a 'barrier to citizenship' (the title of Chapter 5 of her *Citizenship: feminist perspectives*). This third citizenship invites us to reassess the question of sites of bona fide citizenship activity. In doing so, it takes us further than many feminists are prepared to go. Lister, for example, refers approvingly to Anne Phillips' distinction between 'campaigning in public for men to do their fair share of the housework and simply sorting out the division of labour in one's own home' (Lister 1997: 28). The implication is that the former is acting as a citizen and the latter is not, because only public activity can be regarded as citizenship activity. From a post-cosmopolitan point of view, though, such a distinction leads to counter-intuitive conclusions.

In general, indeed, the post-cosmopolitan citizen operates at many different levels of society, and this involves a broader renegotiation of 'the political'. Anne Phillips criticizes Douglas Hurd's late 1980s notion of the 'active citizen', 'who picks up the litter but never gives a thought to the political issues of the day' (Phillips 1991: 84). The word 'litter' is carefully chosen to produce the parody that Phillips wants, but if we replace it with 'waste', an apolitical issue becomes a political one—from an environmental point of view at least. Post-cosmopolitan citizenship is 'strongly in favour of reasserting and re-establishing the importance for modern politics and social life of *"civil society"* (i.e., leaving capitalism aside, the role of voluntarism and the role of family and community)' (Roche 1992: 49; see also Lister 1997: 22). It is therefore opposed to the Rousseauian and Jacobin view that civil society (families, associations, and so on) are a threat to citizenship (see Nisbet 1974: 619, 624, 633–4).

In sum, despite their apparent differences, both liberal and civic republican citizenship subscribe to the view that citizenship is definitionally associated with the public sphere. Post-cosmopolitan citizenship points out, however, that private acts have public implications, and that it is therefore unwise to make the strict public/private distinctions that drive the 'public' view common to both liberal and civic republican citizenship. The second connection between post-cosmopolitan citizenship and the private sphere lies in the arena of virtue. Table 2.1 revealed that liberal and civic republican citizenships are properly distinguished by the former being less driven by the idea of civic virtue than the latter. Emerging post-cosmopolitan citizenship shares a concern with virtue with civic republicanism, but the range of potential citizenship virtues is much wider.

## Citizenship Virtues

In this section, I want to triangulate the content of post-cosmopolitan citizenship virtue by considering its relationship with virtue in liberal and civic republican citizenship. This will involve, first, exploring the claim that liberal citizenship is free of the idea of virtue. I shall conclude that it is not, and that liberal citizenship virtues will form part of any politically legitimate citizenship in modern secular societies. Second, I shall examine the relationship between so-called 'masculine' and 'feminine' virtues, before reasserting the view that what makes a virtue 'citizenly' is its source, or what motivates it, rather than what it actually 'is'. The virtues of post-cosmopolitan citizenship are thus rooted in the kinds of relationship that underpin it, rather than imposed in some more arbitrary fashion.

As for liberal citizenship, then, Derek Heater has pointed out how 'Stephen Macedo has thoroughly demonstrated [that] republicans by no means have a monopoly on civic virtue'

(1999: 32). On Macedo's behalf he goes on:

Freedom, which, after all, is the very essence of liberalism, does not mean a free-for-all: it requires vital moral qualities in the citizen to prevent this abuse. He lists these as: 'tolerance, self-criticism, moderation, and a reasonable degree of engagement in the activities of citizenship'...Essentially, enjoying freedom involves a readiness to uphold and preserve it, and implies an acceptance of the freedom of others. Expressed negatively, apathy and intolerance are the vices abhorred by liberal civic virtue.                    (Heater 1992: 32)

To this list of liberal citizenship virtues, Kymlicka and Norman add 'public reasonableness': 'Liberal citizens must give reasons for their political demands, not just state preferences or make threats' (1994: 366), and Amy Gutman talks of 'mutual respect', since 'Absent mutual respect, citizens cannot be expected to honor the liberal principle of non-discrimination' (1995: 577).

This is an impressive list, and while we might split hairs over which of these dispositions are practices of moral excellence, properly speaking, and which of them are merely admirable qualities or traits, they do enough in combination to undermine the view that liberal citizenship is a virtue-free zone. The point I wish to make, though, is that these virtues can be found in *any* conception of citizenship likely to make headway in the kinds of societies of which I speak here. Put differently, conceptions of citizenship that do not subscribe to public reasonableness, for example, are very unlikely to get a purchase in liberal or social democratic societies. Both the revived civic republican citizenship of recent years, and the post-cosmopolitan citizenship I am developing here, will list public reasonableness in the *desiderata* of virtues for the simple reason that without it they would lack legitimacy. In this connection, Herman van Gunsteren argues that 'virtue is not alien to the civic republic, but it is not the military virtue of the olden days. Rather, it concerns debating, reasonableness, democracy, choice, plurality and carefully limited use of violence' (van Gunsteren 1994: 45).

In his understandable anxiety to include liberal citizenship virtues among those of civic republicanism, van Gunsteren is in danger of losing sight of what is *specific* to civic republican virtue. This is because whatever the specific virtues in civic republican citizenship and post-cosmopolitan citizenship turn out to be, they will only be regarded as legitimately instantiated if they are publicly constituted. In modern liberal and social democratic societies, the 'organic' instantiation of virtues and values—that is to say, instantiation through unexamined tradition—is impossible. For this reason, the virtues of liberal citizenship cannot be used to distinguish this citizenship from other forms because it is present in those other forms.

What is mostly absent from the liberal conception of anything, including liberal citizenship, is the idea of a common good beyond that which emerges from the essentially uncoordinated actions of masses of individuals. Indeed it was the systematic 'public' policy expression of this absence in a succession of New Right administrations under Margaret Thatcher in Britain and Ronald Reagan in the United States in the 1980s that led both left and right, eventually, to wonder whether liberal societies could survive without some ground-level commitment to the idea of 'the public'. In the context of citizenship, this took the form of a debate about the required qualities of individual citizens. Kymlicka and Norman make representative remarks on this debate:

> [M]any classical liberals believed that a liberal democracy could be made secure, even in the absence of an especially virtuous citizenry, by creating checks and balances…Even if each person pursued her own self-interest, without regard for the common good, one set of private interests would check another set of private interests. However, it has become clear that procedural-institutional mechanisms to balance self-interest are not enough, and that some level of civic virtue and public-spiritedness is required.
>
> (Kymlicka and Norman 1994: 359–60)

Once the idea of 'the public' is back on the agenda, and once citizenship is enlisted as a force for reweaving the basic fabric of society, then the civic republican tradition of citizenship becomes an obvious source of inspiration. Civic republicanism has always been committed to the idea of the public and, more specifically, to the idea of the common good. It is in this context that the virtues of civic republican citizenship need to be understood.

The civic republican tradition has its roots in sixth- to fourth-century BC Sparta and Athens, and in Ancient Rome's 500 years of republican rule. As far as citizenship virtue is concerned, for Aristotle, 'the crucial requirement was that citizens must be possessed of and display *aretē*, goodness or virtue. By this Aristotle meant fitting in, in social and political behaviour, to the style of the particular constitution of the *polis*' (Heater 1999: 45). This idea of 'fitting in' is consonant with the notion of members of the *polis* having a common objective towards which to strive, and it being the duty of the citizen to participate actively in the achieving of that objective. This classic civic republican combination of the active citizen contributing to the common good of the polity survives through to the beginnings of its more modern articulation in the work of Machiavelli. Machiavelli regarded *virtù* as the primordial citizen virtue, and while this may appear to take the form of a truism, Derek Heater is right to warn that 'his use of the word *virtù*, though conveniently translated as "virtue", carries many overtones quite absent from the English word' (1999: 48). Bernard Crick, for example, renders *virtù* as 'courage, fortitude, audacity, skill and civic spirit...*virtù* is the quality of mind and action that creates, saves or maintains cities...' (in Heater 1999: 48). In Machiavelli's eyes, cities were worth saving because they embodied the idea of the common good, so once again we see the civic republican connection between citizen virtue and the pursuance of common objectives.

For Machiavelli, says Heater:

The good citizen, effectively educated in the precepts of *virtù*, must lead an active life, whether civilian or military. In civilian life the citizen must take a positive interest in public affairs and, above all, refrain from according priority to a private life of wealth, luxury and ease over a commitment to the general public good. But it is the role of the citizen as soldier that Machiavelli especially emphasizes.

(Heater 1999: 49)

This last sentence is a critical one. Heater points out that the 'Greek word *aretē*, the Latin word *virtus* and the Italian word *virtù* all, significantly, carry in their complexity the meaning of manliness' (Heater 1999: 60). Herman van Gunsteren, too, defines the classical republican citizenship virtues as, '[C]ourage, devotion, military discipline and statecraft' (van Gunsteren 1994: 42), and refers to them as 'masculine'. The idea of the apparent 'masculinity' of civic republican virtue has been so influential that there is an observable tendency to regard any favouring of virtue in the citizenship context with suspicion. In a sharp essay on the subject, Jean Bethke Elshtain refers to the 'dark underside of evocations of civic virtue and the common good' (1986: 100). She claims that '[F]or the great civic republicans of the early modern era...citizens must be prepared to defend civic autonomy through force of arms' (1986: 102–3), and concludes that '[T]he problem with the tradition of civic virtue can be stated succinctly: that virtue is *armed*' (1986: 102). But Elshtain is drawing too general a conclusion from a rather specific case. Having located the original source of her concern in the historical specificity of the civic republican tradition of the early modern era, she draws a general conclusion regarding the 'armed' nature of civic virtue *as such*. We would be better off leaving open the possibility of an unarmed civic virtue, unless and until it becomes clear that civic virtue in all times and all places just has to be masculine in this particular way.

So classically, civic republican virtues were/are those deemed essential to defending and furthering the glory of the republic: courage, leadership, service, sacrifice. These are virtues expressed in the language of conflict, and forged in the earliest days of citizenship: 'the war society of Sparta gave a great deal to the foundation of Western citizenship . . . Spartan citizenship is an intensification of the Athenian notion of public service in that commitment is seen exclusively in life-and-death battlefield terms' (Reisenberg 1992: 7–8). Contemporary attempts to revive the civic republican tradition have presented its supporters with the challenge of maintaining the virtue theme, yet depriving it of unwanted military associations. For the most part this has resulted in some articulation or another of the idea of 'service to the community' as, for example, in Richard Dagger's formulation, part of which I referred to earlier:

As I envision it, civic service includes, but is not confined to, military service. Other forms of service must also be available, and there are many possibilities here, including work as a hospital orderly, a teacher's assistant, an aide to the elderly, or a member of a conservation crew . . . . the point of the service is not to earn a wage or to turn a profit but to do one's duty—to do something for the other members of the community in return for the protection of the law and the other benefits of membership that one has received and hopes to continue to receive. (Dagger 2000: 3)

I talked earlier of 'triangulating' the virtues associated with post-cosmopolitan citizenship, and part of this triangulation involved recognizing the presence of liberal citizenship's 'public reasonableness' in post-cosmopolitan citizenship, without this exhausting the content of its idea of virtue. Now we can say that post-cosmopolitan citizenship virtue shares the idea of a common good with civic republican citizenship, but offers an unarmed account of the virtues necessary for achieving it. In part, this alternative derives from a different account of the key relationships in these citizenships. For civic republicanism, virtue attaches to the relationship between the citizen and the constituted political authority: citizenship virtue here is aimed at 'saving cities'. In our post-cosmopolitan citizenship, virtue attaches to the relations between citizens themselves. Rian Voet points out that '[C]itizenship can, in principle, be both the relationships between a state and an individual citizen and the political relations between citizens themselves' (1998: 9). Most often, contemporary theories of citizenship focus on the former, and this is a direct result of the way in which citizenship is nearly always seen in terms of rights and entitlements. From this point of view the critical relationship is that between the citizen and the state. Post-cosmopolitan citizenship focuses more on the second of Voet's possibilities, and it has rather a particular 'take' on what 'political relations between citizens themselves' might mean. It is no accident that it is feminist examinations of citizenship that have thrown citizen–citizen relations into relief, and therefore no surprise, either, that it is here that the issue of virtue in connection to these relations has been most systematically discussed. At this point the idea of so-called 'feminine' virtues comes into play.

A key framing insight comes from Pnina Werbner and Nira Yuval-Davis: 'rather than a model which posits an opposition between two diametrically opposed approaches—a "liberal" individualist and a "republican" communitarian—feminist scholars seek to formulate models that highlight citizenship and civic activism as dialogical and relational, embedded in cultural and associational life' (1999: 10). The parallel between the idea of post-cosmopolitan citizenship being developed here, and Werbner and Yuval-Davis's 'going beyond' liberal individualism and republican communitarianism should be clear. Our common contention is that a citizenship 'embedded in cultural and associational life' suggests a different set of virtues to those commonly found in the civic republican context. First, then, let me pursue Werbner's understanding of embeddedness and her conclusions regarding citizenship virtue, before saying something about the globalized embeddedness that informs post-cosmopolitan citizenship virtue.

Werbner refers to work by Jennifer Schirmer on 'motherist movements' in Latin America. She writes that these movements 'valorise maternal qualities—caring, compassion, responsibility for the vulnerable—as encompassing and anchored in democratic values' (Werbner 1999: 221). She goes on to suggest that 'political motherhood challenged...established notions of civic legitimacy and created the conditions for the feminisation of citizenship: the reconstitution of citizenship in terms of qualities associated with women's role as nurturers, carers and protectors of the integrity of the family and its individual members' (1999: 221–2). The feminization of citizenship entails, therefore, the establishing of 'caring, compassion, and responsibility for the vulnerable' as citizenship virtues. Kimberly Hutchings suggests that this is precisely what feminist antinuclear campaigners of the 1980s were trying to do, in ways that impinge on how we might conceive and practise global citizenship today:

The campaigners at peace camps such as Greenham Common in England were not simply declaring their presence on the international stage but were also arguing that that international stage should learn from them. The tactics employed at Greenham Common were imbued by the idea of the ethical superiority of the notions of care, connection and responsibility embedded in women's work within the family over the strategic and just-war thinking which could even contemplate the destruction of large swathes of the human race in the pursuit of some greater goal. (Hutchings 2002: 57)

This kind of language will make many people very nervous. Not least, some feminists will worry that such a model runs into the problem of 'essentialism'. Pnina Werbner, for one, is quick to distance herself from such criticism, claiming that these virtues are those associated with women's *role* as carers, rather than with women *as women*—and this is clear in Hutchings, too, above. She does not, therefore, subscribe to the second wave feminist view that these virtues are either possessed uniquely by women and/or that they are superior to those normally associated with 'masculine' roles. She writes that '[P]olitical motherhood as conceived here rests on an encompassing relationship: women are responsible to their families and the political community in its entirety, including men, with regard to issues of universal and humanitarian concern' (1999: 226). The intention here is to make these virtues as much a part of public political life as those, such as public reasonableness, that are already valuably present there. As Werbner says:

[T]he strength of political motherhood as an evolving social movement has been to introduce new human qualities into the public sphere, and to define them as *equally* foundational in the legitimation of the political community. The point is not thus whether men are compassionate and loyal or women rational and objective; the point is that *all* these qualities embody and objectify the ideal of citizenship and their *absence* delegitimises the state and its political authority. It is in this sense that I speak, somewhat ironically (without subscribing to essentialist definitions of intrinsic male and female qualities), of the 'feminisation' of citizenship.                    (Werbner 1999: 227)

The value of the exportation of such qualities into the public sphere is endorsed in many feminist reflections on citizenship. Rian Voet, for example, glosses Jean Bethke Elshtain's argument for the importance of the 'translation to the public sphere of the concerns of the private sphere, and in particular those connected to the protection of children and other vulnerable people' (1998: 14), and Selma Sevenhuijesen argues that:

a feminist ethics of care can have a place in such a conception of citizenship . . . . If we integrate values derived from the ethics of care, such as attentiveness, responsiveness and responsibility, into concepts of citizenship this will produce a dual transformational effect: the concept of citizenship will be enriched and thus better able to cope with diversity and plurality, and care will be 'de-romanticized', enabling us to consider its values as political virtues.

(Sevenhuijesen 1998: 15)

Thus caring is at present generally a gendered activity, and its politicization would involve degendering it: to reclaim it as a citizenly, rather than a gendered, virtue.

This will worry feminists (and others) who balk at the idea of 'female' values and the notion of 'feminizing' public life (even in inverted commas), and it will also worry those who believe that citizenship is definitionally about the public sphere, and that it is definitionally *not* about care and compassion. This latter view is most fiercely held by Michael Ignatieff, who writes that 'the pell-mell retreat from the language of justice to the language of caring is perhaps the most worrying sign of the decadence of the language of citizenship among all parties to the left of Mrs Thatcher' (in Rees 1995: 321), and that 'the language of citizenship is not properly about compassion at all' (Ignatieff 1991: 34).

As I said in an earlier section, though, this confuses the nature of obligations with their source. We should not arbitrarily proclaim some virtues to be citizenly and others not. A more fruitful approach is to consider the source of obligation. If that source can be regarded as political rather than more broadly humanitarian (in the sense of charitable), then as a general rule of thumb the virtues required for meeting that obligation will be properly described as citizenly virtues. Ignatieff offers no clear reason why compassion should not be part of the language of citizenship, except to say that 'compassion is a private virtue which cannot be legislated or enforced' (1991: 34). This is beside the point, since not many will argue that *public* virtues can—or should be—legislated or enforced either. The point is not whether the virtue of compassion is enforceable or not, but whether it is appropriate as a way of meeting the obligations that arise through the kinds of embeddedness that give rise to citizenship. Feminist analyses suggest that it is. Ignatieff would do well, then, to reflect on Pnina Werbner's reminder that '[N]ot only feminism but socialism, anti-racism or multiculturalism introduce new human qualities—of economic egalitarianism, tolerance or the right to cultural recognition—into the discourses of legitimation that permeate the public sphere. These new values continuously reconstitute what it means to be a citizen' (1999: 227).

In post-cosmopolitan citizenship, then, the distinction between the good person and the good citizen has not disappeared. Over two thousand years ago Aristotle asked whether 'the excellence of the good man and that of the good citizen are identical or different' (1946: 101/1276b). He concluded that they 'are not in *all* cases identical' (1946: 103/1277a) because 'the excellence of the citizen must be an excellence relative to the constitution. It follows on from this that if there are several different types of constitution...there cannot be a single absolute excellence of the good citizen' (1946: 101–2/1276b). In Aristotelian terms, therefore, Michael Ignatieff is right to say that 'Germans who stood by while their Jewish neighbors were deported were "good citizens"', but wrong to continue that 'Aristotle had not envisaged a situation in which a good citizen was not also a good man' (1995: 62). Aristotle is quite clear that the condition of citizenship is different from the condition of 'humanity', and this is reflected in the distinctive virtues associated with each condition. This has its analogue in my conception of the different kinds of relationship that give rise to humanitarian obligations on the one hand, and to citizenship obligations on the other.

Let me now draw these threads together in the context of post-cosmopolitan citizenship. We have seen distinctions drawn between the virtues of liberal, civic republican ('masculine'), and feminist citizenship. The point now is precisely *not* to plump for one or another of these types of virtue and arbitrarily say that *those* are the virtues of post-cosmopolitan citizenship. The determinant is not 'virtues themselves' but the relationships that give rise to citizenship obligations. Then it is a question of determining which virtues are best suited to meeting those obligations. This enables us, importantly, to distinguish citizenship from other types of human condition and relation, but no longer on the arbitrary basis of saying that some virtues are 'citizenly' and some are more broadly 'humanitarian'. Citizenship is a relationship of strangers, which is why the embeddedness of families, for example, does not give rise to citizenship-type obligations. In Lichtenberg's terms, relationships between strangers can be 'moral' or 'historical'. A moral relationship is like that between the Good Samaritan and the poor unfortunate on the side of the road. The Samaritan had nothing to do with the man's plight, but he was in a position to alleviate it. This is a neighbourly act, not an act of citizenship. A 'historical' relationship between strangers is one involving, as we saw, some 'antecedent action, undertaking, agreement, relationship, or the like' (Lichtenberg 1981: 81). This kind of relationship can give rise to citizenship obligations, and then the question is which virtues are best suited to meeting those obligations. This means that public reasonableness, courage, care, compassion, and justice might *all* be regarded as citizenship virtues.

At the very beginning of this chapter I spoke of the shortcomings of analyses of citizenship that relied on static packages of the concepts that make up citizenship. The insistence that care and compassion cannot be citizenship virtues seems to me to be one example of this kind of shortcoming. Identification of these virtues as potentially citizenship virtues does not take us 'outside' citizenship. Those who believe that it does are effectively confounding the nature of citizenship virtues with what prompts them in the first place.

## Territorial and Non-territorial Citizenship

Both liberal and civic republican notions of citizenship are 'territorial', which is to say that citizenship is associated with membership of a defined, usually contiguous, political space. The historical record speaks, though, of notions of 'world' and 'cosmopolitan' citizenship that do not fit the dominant territorial model, and any full account of the citizenship experience must have room for this possibility. Of course, territoriality 'means' different things in liberal and civic republican citizenship, and in this regard a contrast between the two can be properly drawn. For the former, territoriality is important because of the rights and entitlements that go with membership of the relevant territory: 'Citizenship may be defined as that set of practices (juridical, political, economic and cultural) which define a person as a competent member of society, and which as a consequence shape the flow of resources to persons and social groups' (Turner 1993*b*: 2).

For republican citizenship, membership of a specified political territory is less to do with entitlements and more to do with duty and/or responsibility. Turner, again, writes on citizenship in republican Rome in the following terms: 'Within this social context, the notion of citizenship rights had a very circumscribed significance, being the status of (rational) property owners who had certain public duties and responsibilities within the city-state' (Turner 1990: 202). But while liberal and republican citizenships can be distinguished by their emphasis on rights and entitlements, and on duties and responsibilities, respectively, they *share* the territorial basis for deciding the distribution of rights and responsibilities.

It is worth connecting this observation with another feature common to both liberal and republican versions of citizenship: they are both discriminatory. Citizenship is a condition for which one requires qualifications, and those who do not qualify in the relevant ways are denied it. In this sense, citizenship is a good that is distributed and, as in any regime of social justice, its distribution is, by definition, discriminatory. As Peter Reisenberg points out, 'citizenship has been an ambiguous institution throughout history and... it has been compatible with many forms of political organization. From the beginning it has meant privilege and exclusion; it is no exaggeration to say that one of its principal functions has been as an agent or principle of discrimination' (1992: p. xvii). Gerard Delanty accurately echoes this point: 'from the very beginning the term [citizenship] entails exclusion since not everyone is in possession of it . . . . No account of citizenship can evade the fact that it was originally constructed in order to exclude and subordinate people' (2000: 11). It is, by contrast, most certainly not the case that ' "Citizenship" is a technical term in moral and political philosophy that entails a particular set of democratic relationships' (Light 2002: 158).

A question for us is whether citizenship is *by definition* discriminatory. If we regard the liberal/republican distinction as a comprehensive 'take' on citizenship possibilities, then we might be tempted to answer 'yes', since they both have discrimination at their heart. This seems to be the idea at work in Anthony Rees's affirmation that 'there are problems with citizenship in any of its varieties: it is less inclusive a concept, even in theory, than many have thought, and needs to be buttressed by something external to it, namely sentiments of benevolence towards non-citizens and whose citizenship is incomplete' (Rees 1995: 313). Rees's point is that benevolence, with its countervailing sense of inclusion, is a sentiment that lies outside citizenship, although he does leave open the alternative possibility: '[A] generalised sense of benevolence is necessary for the mutual obligations of citizenship to be respected' (1995: 323). Let us record for now, then, the possibility of a citizenship 'beyond discrimination'—and, by the same token, beyond territory and its close cousin, membership.

The contemporary revival of interest in citizenship is driven in large measure by two mutually reinforcing considerations and one seismic demographic fact. The two considerations are, first, that citizenship is dominantly conceived in terms of membership of a nation-state and, second, that since the Second

World War at least, it has been regarded as centrally about the claiming of entitlements. The seismic demographic fact is that more people are on the move across the world today than throughout the whole of human history. Most of these people are moving (or trying to move) in the direction of societies that are better off—societies that, in citizenship-speak, can offer better entitlements than the countries of origin of these 'economic migrants'. I said earlier that such has been the dominance of the rights and entitlements view of citizenship over the past 50 years that it is sometimes hard to conceive of it in terms of duties and responsibilities, and much the same might be said of the way in which citizenship is regarded as being centrally about membership of a nation-state.

It has not always been thus. Derek Heater is only half right when he writes that 'The assumption that citizenship is a singular, bilateral relationship between the individual and the state is deeply embedded in our understanding of the concept. It is a model common to both classical Greek and modern nationalist thinking on the subject' (1999: 115). He is right that the individual–state relationship has practically become reified in citizenship theory, but wrong to imply that this has always been the case. In classical Greek times there was no 'state' in the sense we understand it today, so Andrew Linklater is nearer the mark than Heater: 'Traditional perspectives maintain that modern conceptions of citizenship are anchored in the world of the bounded community; they contend that it loses its precise meaning when divorced from territoriality, sovereignty and shared nationality' (1998*b*: 23). The idea of a 'bounded community' leaves open the question of the *type* of community, and while this may be the contemporary nation-state, the historical record suggests that it does not have to be. We will all agree, for example, that the ancient Greek city-state can properly be regarded as a site where citizenship was granted and exercised. Then Peter Reisenberg points to how, at a later historical moment, 'citizenship became possible as an institution in the

Middle Ages only when a certain level of economic activity had been reached. That level presupposes the existence of a physical city of some size, the regular use of money in trade and eventually banking, specialization of labor, and at least some craft or industrial activity' (1992: 110). Reisenberg's implicit point is that we should look for the socio-economic conditions that give rise to citizenship, rather than any particular size or sort of 'container' in which citizenship is practised. During the medieval period and after, these socio-economic conditions existed most evidently at the level of the town or city. Indeed in historical terms the municipality has been at the heart of citizenship practice for much longer than the modern nation-state. As Derek Heater observes, the 'very etymology of the word reveals its association with a city—in English, in French (*citoyen*), in Italian (*cittadino*), in German (*Bürger*), for example' (1999: 134). Those who would now argue that the modern nation-state is definitionally the centre of gravity of citizenship, and that therefore cosmopolitan or international citizenship simply make no sense, should perhaps look at the way in which the idea of bona fide sites of citizenship activity have *evolved* over the years: 'For two hundred years citizenship and nationality have been political Siamese twins. Before the late eighteenth century the relationship was much looser than we have been accustomed to assume, and the connection is loosening again in our own age as multiple and world citizenships become increasingly evident' (Heater 1999: 95).

In fact what we find in the historical record is not so much evolution, as the coexistence of competing views as to the proper realm or sphere of citizenship practice. In this regard, Gerard Delanty comments that 'An identification with cosmopolitan community has always been a central feature of western thought ever since the Greeks made a cosmic myth of their civilization. The identification of the early church with the universal community of humanity continued the Roman aspiration for world empire' (2000: 53). Heater supports this view, suggesting that Greek and Roman Stoics argued for 'the conception of the oneness of mankind and the existence of a universal Natural Law', while 'Belief in the moral value of cosmopolitanism was resuscitated by the classical revivals of the Renaissance and Enlightenment. Eighteenth-century writers and intellectuals—the likes of Voltaire, Franklin and Paine were proud to own the title of "world citizen" ' (1999: 135). More particularly, Delanty goes on, 'It was not until Immanuel Kant that cosmopolitanism became linked with citizenship. Kant opened the first great modern debate on cosmopolitan citizenship around a notion of an international order based upon civil society' (Delanty 2000: 54). Crucially, Delanty comments, 'His [i.e. Kant's] was a cosmopolitanism of spirit and intellect—*it had no relation to space*' (2000: 55; emphasis added). So if Michael Walzer is right to say, as I suspect he is, that 'A citizen is, most simply, a member of a political commun-ity, entitled to whatever prerogatives and encumbered with whatever responsibilities are attached to membership' (1989: 211), we should not necessarily assume that this political community is a bounded, or even a 'real', one. As Maurice Roche says, 'We need to remind ourselves that citizenship is not reducible to membership of the modern nation-state. It is not primarily definable as "national citizenship" . . . citizenship is mainly definable in terms of the existence of a political community, civil society and public sphere, whether or not that is coterminous with a nation-state' (1995: 726). This notion of the 'public sphere' is critical, as will shortly become apparent.

So the answer to Derek Heater's orientating question: 'Has citizenship as a state-defined status outlived its usefulness?' (1999: 160), is surely 'yes'. The truth is that citizenship has only been state-defined for a relatively short period of the history of the concept. As long as states exist, of course, citizenship will quite properly continue to be associated with them, but to associate it *exclusively* with the nation-state would be both to fly in the face of the historical evidence and to ignore the changing conditions under which citizenship is, or may be, presently exercised. Put differently, if citizenship *were* definitionally associated with the nation-state, one would have expected a decline in its (citizenship's) importance, mirroring the way in which nation-states have leaked power and authority, both upwards and downwards, in recent years. In fact, though, the opposite has happened, reflecting in part the repercussions of the demographic changes I mentioned above, but also the notion that citizenship still makes sense as an idea under these changing conditions.

We are left, though, with the more general form of Heater's question, which he expresses as follows: 'A citizen was, as originally conceived, a full member of a *polis* or *civitas*, a single, coherent political body. Because the environment in which the citizen has been expected to operate has been dramatically diversified, has citizenship perforce so adaptively evolved that it has lost its true essence?' (1999: 157). In other words, even though we might accept that the nation-state is too narrow a frame of reference for contemporary citizenship, we still might believe that the presence and identification of a 'single, coherent political body' within which to claim the rights and exercise the responsibilities of citizenship is definitionally essential. If this is right, then cosmopolitan citizenship, or any other conception of citizenship that follows the rubric of cosmopolitan citizenship, such as the post-cosmopolitan citizenship under development here, seems theoretically unworkable.

Once again, though, if 'single, coherent political bodies' ever existed—a disputable claim in itself—then they certainly do not now. As Delanty puts it: 'The state is no longer entirely in command of all the forces that shape it and sovereignty has been eroded both downwards to subnational units, such as cities and regions, and upwards to transnational agencies, such as the European Union' (2000: 19). If, then, 'single, coherent political bodies' are the conceptual and practical precondition for the existence of citizenship, we can only draw the conclusion that citizenship is dead. A more appropriate reaction, though, is to focus on the *multiplicity* of 'political bodies' of which people in late modernity are (potentially) members, and to consider what citizenship might look like under these conditions. Along the way, we should take seriously the idea that these political bodies need not be 'real', but may be 'discursive'.

The first disruption of nation-state-centred citizenship works along the lines of Delanty's comments, above. Thus even the most ardent supporter of the view that citizenship is tied in some fundamental sense to modern nation-states must surely recognize the incipient citizenship that goes along with development of the European Union (e.g. Falk 2002: 23–6). In the context of the European Union, transnational citizenship is a reality, although one can only guess at the rights and obligations of future EU citizenship, ineluctably bound up as they are with complex debates about how European integration will, and should, develop.

Transnational citizenship of this type is still a *territorial* citizenship, however, and therefore does not have the mark of *non-territoriality* that I see as definitive of post-cosmopolitan citizenship (see Table 2.1). At this point it is worth recalling remarks made earlier regarding the nature of the relationships at the heart of the 'new' citizenships I am describing here. Both liberal and civic republican citizenships focus on the relationship between the citizen and the constituted political authority—a 'vertical' relationship, if you will. This is also true of the transnational citizenship I described in the previous paragraph. On the other hand, cosmopolitan citizenship, some forms of feminist citizenship, and the post-cosmopolitan citizenship I am developing here, all focus on the relationships *between citizens*. This brings into relief another phenomenon often associated with an increasingly globalized world: the idea of a 'global civil society'. Civil society has always been associated with citizenship: the sum total of voluntary associations outside the formal political institutions of the machinery of the state in which people act in the public sphere. Civil society is where citizens interact with each other as citizens, and as the nation-state has haemorrhaged power and authority both within and without, and as the transnational nature of many contemporary political challenges has become more obvious, the idea— and indeed perhaps the fact—of a transnational civil society has come into being. The most obvious manifestations of this occur in opposition to the major set-pieces of international politics and finance, such as the G8 and World Trade Organization meetings. Seattle, Prague, Quebec, and Gothenburg have already entered activist folklore as explosions of global citizenship activity, and who knows how many more names will need to be added to the list. These *événements* are the tip of an iceberg of global citizenship activity: 'These networks of transnational activity conceived both as a project and as a preliminary reality are producing a new orientation towards political identity and community, what cumulatively can be described as global civil society' (Falk 1994: 138). International non-governmental organizations (INGOs) are often regarded as performing a similar function (Linklater 2002: 326). Such networks and organizations, and the kind of civil society they engender, are non-territorial, and are thus a foundation of the non-territoriality that I see as a key defining feature of our post-cosmopolitan citizenship.

It is important, then, to distinguish between 'big territoriality' and 'non-territoriality'. European Union citizenship is an example of the former, while the citizenship associated with a nascent global civil society is an example of the latter. In truth, 'big territorial' citizenship has been around for a very long time. As J. L. Cohen recognizes of Alexander's empire, for example, '[I]t was then that the concept of citizenship, which had its historical origin, of course, in the self-government of urban communities, began to be applied to a context of relationships much wider than that existing within a city-state'

(1954: 73). Cohen goes on to indicate the conceptual gap between 'big' and 'non-territorial' citizenship by commenting that, when Alexander died and political unity dissipated, 'the only world society in which a single citizenship seemed reasonable was a metaphorical one' (1954: 73). To call this a 'metaphorical' citizenship, though, is perhaps to make it sound less real than it actually was. The Stoics, for example, 'asserted... the ultimate moral equality of all human beings' (Reisenberg 1992: 53), and this had a profound and very real effect later on Roman and, particularly, Christian understandings of citizenship—in which loyalty to the universal Heavenly City replaced loyalty to the particular earthly one.

In contemporary citizenship theory, the theme of nonterritorial citizenship is taken up most explicitly by those who endorse what has come to be known as 'cosmopolitan citizenship'. This idea has developed in self-conscious opposition to what its supporters regard as outdated statist conceptions of citizenship. Such supporters are 'critical of statist approaches which deny that citizenship can be attached to any arrangements other than the nation-state' (Linklater 1998: 29). It will be clear by now that this is a characteristic feature of 'postcosmopolitan citizenship', too. As we have seen, one way of building a conception of citizenship 'beyond the state' is to consider the various emergent forms of transnational citizenship, such as those associated with membership of the European Union. We have also canvassed the possibility of a 'global civil society' in which the idea and practice of global citizenship might make sense. Cosmopolitan citizenship, however, might also be seen as a distant cousin of the 'metaphorical' citizenship referred to above by Cohen, in which the idea of a global 'public sphere' replaces, or in some cases complements, the idea of a global 'civil society'. Thus, for Gerard Delanty, a

central dimension to this conception of citizenship is a sense of citizenship as multi-levelled, cutting across the subnational, the national and the transnational, for citizenship can no longer be located exclusively on any one level. One of the main critical contributions of this book [i.e. his book] is a defence of the idea of a *cosmopolitan public sphere* while being more critical of the prospect of a *cosmopolitan civil society*. (Delanty 2000: 5)

In the capable hands of Andrew Linklater, this idea of a global public sphere is deployed precisely in order to head off the criticism that cosmopolitan citizenship is not a citizenship at all. In the following lengthy, but key, quotation, Linklater effectively puts the case he wants to oppose, echoing points we saw John Horton make earlier:

Appealing to cosmopolitan citizenship may inspire fellow nationals to honour obligations to peoples elsewhere, but this distorts the notion of citizenship in their view. From their standpoint, to be a citizen is to have concrete rights against, and duties to, a specific sovereign state rather than voluntary and inexact duties to the rest of humanity; it is to belong to a bounded political community which enjoys the right of collective self-determination, and which can decide who can enter its ranks and who can be turned away; it is to have a special bond with others who decide together whether to accept onerous moral obligations to outsiders and how to discharge the duties they impose upon themselves. Citizens therefore enjoy privileges as members of sovereign states which aliens do not have, and cannot claim on the grounds of sheer humanity...Traditional approaches argue that appeals to cosmopolitan citizenship amount to little more than an exercise in moral exhortation while the nation-state is the dominant form of political community. Their contention is that the idea of world citizenship may have considerable moral force, but, on any strict definition of citizenship, the term is self-evidently and unalterably oxymoronic.

(Linklater 1998*b*: 23–4)

In other words, 'Critics of world citizenship protest that its exhortatory and rhetorical purposes are entirely divorced from the Aristotelian idea of active involvement in the democratic public sphere' (Linklater 1998*b*: 27). Not so, says Linklater. For him, 'involvement in the democratic public sphere' can take many forms, and one of them is political argumentation. In Linklater's view, the 'central aim' of cosmopolitan citizenship is the liberal one of ensuring that 'dialogue and consent' replace force as the means by which disputes are settled in the international arena (1998*b*: 25). He goes on to claim that '[I]t requires political action to build communication communities in which outsiders, and especially the most vulnerable among them, have the power to "refuse and negotiate offers" and to contest unjust social structures' (1998*b*: 25). As we saw in Chapter 1, Linklater calls this a 'dialogic' approach to citizenship, according to which the central citizenship idea of involvement in the public sphere is not abandoned, but rather recast in the non-territorial context of an incipient discursive democracy. This seems genuinely non-territorial, in the same sense that an epistemic community, or a community of the diaspora, is non-territorial.

By deploying the dialogical idea, then, Linklater hopes to have headed off one kind of criticism of cosmopolitan citizenship, but there is another. It is clear from the long quotation above that Linklater is sensitive to the charge that the duties of citizenship are quite precise—that 'to be a citizen is to have concrete rights against, and duties to, a specific sovereign state rather than voluntary and inexact duties to the rest of humanity'. He is sensitive, in other words, to the kinds of criticism we saw Michael Ignatieff making earlier regarding the importation of *ethical* notions such as care and compassion into what is fundamentally a *political* conception. As Linklater puts it: '[T]he argument is that, if it is to have any real meaning, cosmopolitan citizenship must involve rather more than moral commitments not to exploit the weaknesses of others—more than the ethical resolution to treat all other human beings with care and compassion' (1998*b*: 28). Linklater accepts this criticism and once again, the discursive, or dialogical, moment in cosmopolitan citizenship is enlisted to resist it. Linklater's contention seems to be that the commitment to dialogue and discussion is somehow more 'political' than the commitment to care and compassion. So he says that while '[W]orld citizenship may embody commitments to treat the vulnerable with compassion...it must also embrace the principle of engaging others as equals within wider communities of discourse' (1998*b*: 34).

In its own terms, Linklater's response to Ignatieff is sound, accepting as it does a standard distinction between the 'ethical' and the 'political', and showing how his (Linklater's) conception of cosmopolitan citizenship is political rather than ethical. But Linklater is then in danger of being outflanked by those who would question his understanding of 'political'. Why, we might ask, is 'engaging others as equals within wider communities of discourse' a 'political' notion, while 'the ethical resolution to treat all other human beings with care and compassion', is not? They both share the key citizenship idea of active involvement in the public sphere, so the only difference can be that the activity of 'discourse' is somehow more political than the activity of care and compassion. But this is open to the feminist objection that we should pause before consigning apparently 'private' practices and virtues to the category of the non-political. From this point of view, the determination to regard care and compassion as non-political virtues is ideological rather than analytical.

Another Linklater objection appears to be that care and compassion are owed too broadly (their 'non-specificity'). But this cannot work for him, since the point, precisely, of cosmopolitan citizenship is to urge us towards the idea that the obligations of citizenship extend beyond the nation-state. In all, it may be that Linklater is giving too much ground to his critics by seeking to 'shore up' the world citizen's commitment to treat the vulnerable with care and compassion with the somehow more political—and therefore more citizenly—principle of dialogical equality. As I have suggested, the starting-point should not be 'which virtues are citizenly?', but 'what kinds of relationship give rise to citizenship obligations?'. This leaves open the question of which virtues are best suited to meeting those obligations.

## Cosmopolitan and Post-cosmopolitan Citizenship

All the foregoing suggests the need to distinguish carefully between cosmopolitan and post-cosmopolitan citizenship and to make sure we are clear about the differences between them. Certainly cosmopolitan citizenship, as articulated by Linklater and others, shares its non-territoriality with post-cosmopolitan citizenship. Both of them are also embarked on 'the quest for a new language of politics which challenges the belief that the individual's central political obligations are to the nation state' (Linklater 2002: 317). But on the other hand we have remarked cosmopolitanism's reluctance to entertain care and compassion as potential citizenship virtues, and this is a key aspect of post-cosmopolitan citizenship. Similarly, cosmopolitanism's non-territoriality seems to be accompanied by the belief that citizenship is carried out exclusively in the public sphere, a view that is again challenged by post-cosmopolitan citizenship.

Yet it is perhaps in regard to the feature that they seem most obviously to have in common that they turn out to differ most—non-territoriality. In this context, Kimberly Hutchings percep-tively points to two types of conception of non-territoriality, and argues for a citizenship that 'rather than ... being incorpo-rated in an ethical universalism which is latent in concepts of liberal-democratic citizenship ... becomes located in the actual interrelation and interaction of both individuals and collectives' (1996: 127). Towards the end of Chapter 1 I suggested that both 'dialogic' and 'distributive' cosmopol-itanism share a thin and non-material account of the ties that bind members of the cosmopolitan community together. This tie is 'some vision of a universal community of humankind' (Linklater 2002: 317)—the 'ethical universalism' to which Hutchings refers. In contrast, in Chapter 1, and again here,

I argued that post-cosmopolitan citizenship's 'community' is created by the 'historical' or (better) 'always already' obligations of globalization. This differs markedly from the ideal and discursive boundaries of cosmopolitanism in its (post-cosmopolitanism's) rooting of the space of citizenship in 'global actualities rather than transcendent principles' (Hutchings 1996: 128). As I explained in Chapter 1, post-cosmopolitanism's obligation space is ' "produced" by the activities of individuals and groups with the capacity to spread and impose themselves in geographical [and] diachronic . . . space'. This produced space has no determinate size (it is not a city, or a state, and nor is it even 'universal') since its scope varies with the case. In this context it is worth pointing out that cosmopolitan citizenship is sometimes criticized for implying obligations that are too demanding in scope and extent because of its references to a 'community which includes all humankind' (Linklater 2002: 323). Post-cosmopolitanism's rootedness in identifiable relations of actual harm, in contrast, limits obligations to those implicit in these relations. These may still be extensive and demanding, as in the case of the obligations generated by the phenomenon of global warming. But this very example makes it clear that the obligations are not those of 'all humankind' since not all humankind contributes unsustainably to global warming.

The principal difference between cosmopolitan and post-cosmopolitan citizenship, then, is that between the 'thin' community of common humanity and the 'thick' community of 'historical obligation'. I shall have further opportunities to comment on these issues in Chapter 3, in the specific context of the example of ecological citizenship.

## Conclusion

In this chapter I have sought to redeem the prospectus outlined in its first paragraph: that a new description of citizenship is required to cope with ideological and material changes that are taking place in the world today. It was part of my intention to show that this new citizenship—which I have called 'post-cosmopolitan citizenship'—cannot be fully expressed in either traditional liberal or civic republican ways, or in the more recent cosmopolitan idiom. The principal characteristics of post-cosmopolitan citizenship are the non-reciprocal nature of the obligations associated with it, the non-territorial yet material nature of its sense of political space, its recognition that this political space should include the private as well as the public realm, and, relatedly, its focus on virtue and its determination to countenance the possibility of 'private' virtues being virtues of citizenship. I also said in the first paragraph of the chapter that post-cosmopolitan citizenship has a quite specific articulation in the guise of environmental politics, and so it is to ecological citizenship that I now turn.

# Chapter 3

# Ecological Citizenship

Chapter 2 was about a new type of citizenship that can be neither discursively nor politically contained within the two dominant citizenship forms, liberal and republican. I described a 'post-cosmopolitan' citizenship that differs from both these forms, as well as from current attempts to move beyond them in the guise of cosmopolitan citizenship. At the beginning of Chapter 2, I mentioned a phenomenon that gives rise to post-cosmopolitan citizenship's 'most precise articulation': environmental politics. The present chapter is devoted to spelling out this articulation in the form of what I shall call 'ecological citizenship'.

Hartley Dean makes some useful orientating remarks as far as the connections between environmental politics and citizenship are concerned:

Green thinking has impacted on our understandings of citizenship in at least three different ways. First, environmental concerns have entered our understanding of the rights we enjoy as citizens. Second, the enhanced level of global awareness associated with ecological thinking has helped to broaden our understanding of the potential scope of citizenship. Third, emergent ecological concerns have added fuel to a complex debate about the responsibilities that attach to citizenship. (Dean 2001: 491)

Dean draws our attention, first, to the issue of environmental rights. I shall say something more about this shortly, but most of us are at least vaguely aware that environmental rights have been canvassed as an addition to the standard triumvirate of civil, political, and social rights, although there is some debate as to whether they *are* indeed an addition, or simply a subset of one of the traditional group. It is commonly argued, for example, that the environmental rights are a type of social right rather than something completely different. However that may be, we know from Chapter 2 that citizenship is in part about the defining and claiming of rights against the state, so Dean is merely drawing our attention to a rather obvious— but still important—connection between citizenship and environmentalism.

Second, Dean mentions the global nature of (some) environmental problems. In Chapter 2, I suggested that the phenomenon of globalization prompts the question of whether citizenship can be conceived beyond the state. It only does so if we can move beyond liberal and civic republican conceptions of citizenship, both of which are defined by their 'stateness'. Cosmopolitan citizenship is one type of answer to the question of whether there can be a citizenship beyond the state, and post-cosmopolitan citizenship is another. In this chapter I shall argue that Dean's 'global awareness associated with ecological thinking' is of a type much better suited to post-cosmopolitan citizenship than to its cosmopolitan cousin.

Third, Dean refers to the way in which ecological concerns have given rise to talk of responsibilities as well as rights. The social objective to which these responsibilities relate is the 'sustainable society', and the questions posed by environmental politics are: what kinds of responsibilities relate to this object-ive, and to whom or what are they owed? These are citizenship-type questions, and the answers to them in the ecological context take us beyond liberal and civic republican citizenship, and past cosmopolitan citizenship.

## The Story So Far

The self-evident nature of Dean's remarks might lead us to think that the citizenship–environment connection would be a well-explored one, so it is a major surprise to find how little systematic work has been done on the issue. John Barry (1999, 2002), Mark Smith (1998), and Peter Christoff (1996) have made important inroads, though, and Angel Valencia (2002) has given us a critically comprehensive survey of the territory. Barry argues strongly for the idea of virtue in ecological politics, and it will be clear from Chapter 2 that this opens up the pos-sibility of a rather particular conception of environmental or ecological citizenship in the tradition of civic republicanism. I shall explore this possibility in detail below, pointing out that while Barry certainly heads in the right direction, we will only reach his required destination through post-cosmopolitan citizenship rather than one of the other more traditional forms.

Mark Smith, likewise, importantly refers to a 'new politics of obligation', according to which 'human beings have obligations to animals, trees, mountains, oceans, and other members of the biotic community' (1998: 99). I am not sure that all of these obligations (or rather to whom or to what he says they are owed) are obligations of citizenship properly speaking, and I shall have more to say on this later. But the idea of obligation to which he refers is certainly central to what I would regard as a defensible articulation of ecological citizenship, and the word should immediately alert us to Table 2.1 where our three types of citizenship are set out. 'Obligation' and 'responsibility' are not, it will be remembered, the language of liberal citizenship, so it is unlikely that the type of citizenship to which Smith refers will lend itself to full expression in the liberal idiom. As he says, 'At the centre of this intellectual project is the firm conviction that conventional conceptions of justice and citizenship do not provide the human species with an adequate set of tools for resolving the difficulties created by ecological damage today' (1998: 91). I hope to build on Smith's valuable insights in what follows.

Another key contribution has been made by Peter Christoff. It will be remembered that one of the definitional questions raised in the citizenship context is whether there can be a citizenship 'beyond the state'. We have seen that both cosmopolitans and post-cosmopolitans think that there can, and that the former believe that one of the reasons this is so is because citizenship is about participation in the public sphere, and that there is no reason to confine this sphere to the state. Christoff makes a useful contrast in this context: 'it is helpful to look at notions of citizenship from a completely different angle, and turn to conceptions of citizenship based on moral responsibility and participation in the public sphere rather than those defined formally by legal relationships to the state' (1996: 157). He picks up the transnational nature of many environmental problems and locates these in globalizing developments of which they are both a symptom and a cause. Such developments, he argues, 'emphasise the growing disjuncture or dislocation observed earlier between moral citizenship (as practised in individual and "community" action and moral responsibility) and legal citizenship as defined by the nation-state' (1996: 161). This dislocation survives in—and indeed nurtures— the idea of ecological citizenship that I develop later in this chapter.

The value of Barry's, Smith's, and Christoff's work lies in seeing that there is more to be said about the relationship between citizenship and the environment than can be said from the dominant liberal and territorial point of view. Bart van Steenbergen, in contrast, has devoted a widely quoted essay to this relationship (van Steenbergen 1994*b*). He builds on T. H. Marshall's influential three-fold typology of citizenship (civil, political, and social citizenship) in the following way: 'It is my intention to explore the possibility that at the edge of the twenty-first century, citizenship will gain a new and fourth dimension. I am referring here to the notion of ecological citizenship as an addition, but also as a correction, to the three existing forms of citizenship: civil, political and social' (van Steenbergen 1994*b*: 142). The idea of environmental rights in the citizenship context is indeed very important, but over-reliance on Marshall could prevent us from seeing what is genuinely interesting in the environment–citizenship relationship. As we know, Marshall's is notoriously a rights-based typology, yet as Smith, for example, rightly points out, one of environmental politics' most crucial contributions to contemporary theorizing is its focus on duties and obligations. van Steenbergen's use of Marshall as an organizing framework makes him miss this, and his implicitly affirmative answer to the question of whether Marshall's typology can cope with current developments is given too hastily (van Steenbergen 1994*a*: 3).

Similarly, the promise of Fred Twine's decision to devote one whole part of his book on citizenship (1994) to the theme of 'environmental interdependence' rather evaporates as, instead of telling us what environmental or ecological citizenship might actually be about and comparing and contrasting it with other sorts of citizenship, he merely points out that the redemption of Marshallian social rights claims is more problematic than ever due to the 'growing environmental and therefore material limits' to the basis for redeeming such claims (Twine 1994: 4). Interesting—and even true—this may be, but to limit the fallout produced by bringing environmentalism and citizenship into contact to this seems to me to be a missed opportunity.

I also think that rights-talk can be a little *too* intoxicating in the context of the environment and citizenship. van Steenbergen himself, for example, makes the giant leap from arguing sensibly for a different *type* of citizenship right to the following rather less convincing idea: 'in short, ecological citizenship... has to do with the extension of citizenship rights to non-human beings' (1994*b*: 146). I shall suggest in more detail later in the chapter why I think it is a mistake to try to extend the citizen community in this way. Briefly, though, it is because I believe citizenship rights to be a matter of justice, and justice can only very arguably be predicated of non-human beings (Dobson 1998: 166–83). I do, though, think that such beings can be moral patients, and therefore must be regarded as members of the moral community. But then our relationships with them are humanitarian rather than citizenly, and so to regard ecological citizenship as extending *citizen* rights to non-human animals is a mistake.

What van Steenbergen and Twine valuably show, though, is that there is *something* to be said about the relationship between citizenship and the environment within the liberal idiom. I would not at all want to be taken to be claiming that liberal citizenship's 'take' on the environment is politically unimportant. My point, rather, is that to try to capture the *entirety* of environment–citizenship relations under the liberal sign is a mistake, since the former will always overflow the latter. It is also my point, of course, that civic republican or cosmopolitan conceptions of citizenship will not do the capturing job either, which is why the post-cosmopolitan framework turns out to be necessary.

## Environmental and Ecological Citizenship

It might have been noticed that so far in this chapter I have been using the terms 'environmental citizenship' and 'ecological citizenship' more or less interchangeably. I want to now introduce a little more precision, and to have these terms refer to quite specific phenomena. From now on I shall take 'environmental citizenship' to refer to the way in which the environment–citizenship relationship can be regarded from a liberal point of view. Referring back to Table 2.1, then, this is a citizenship that deals in the currency of environmental rights, that is conducted exclusively in the public sphere, whose principal virtues are the liberal ones of reasonableness and a willingness to accept the force of the better argument and procedural legitimacy, and whose remit is bounded political configurations modelled on the nation-state. For the most rough-and-ready purposes, it can be taken that environmental citizenship here refers to attempts to extend the discourse and practice of rights-claiming into the environmental context.

I shall reserve the term 'ecological citizenship', on the other hand, for the specifically ecological form of post-cosmopolitan citizenship developed in Chapter 2. At first blush, then, ecological citizenship deals in the currency of non-contractual responsibility, it inhabits the private as well as the public sphere, it refers to the source rather than the nature of responsibility to determine what count as citizenship virtues, it works with the language of virtue, and it is explicitly non-territorial. Once again let me stress that I do not think that ecological citizenship is any more politically worthy or important than its environmental counterpart. From a political point of view, indeed, I regard environmental and ecological citizenship as complementary in that, while they organize themselves on different terrains, they can both plausibly be read as heading in the same direction: the sustainable society. Enshrining environmental rights in constitutions, for example, is as much a part of realizing the political project of sustainability as carrying out ecological responsibilities. And, as Tim Hayward points out, the same applies in reverse:

Certainly, there are many political questions which obviously cannot and should not be dealt with at the constitutional level...there is a strong case for enhancing the democratic capacities of state institutions to respond to new ecological imperatives formulated 'from below'. In particular, this could mean allowing more feedback and input from the associations of civil society.       (Hayward 2001: 129)

I do, though, regard ecological citizenship as more intellectually interesting than environmental citizenship from the point of view of citizenship itself. This is because environmental citizenship (understood, now, in the rather more specific sense I outlined in the paragraph above) leaves citizenship unchanged, in that the environment–citizenship encounter can be exhaustively captured and described by its liberal variant. Ecological citizenship, on the other hand, obliges us to rethink the traditions of citizenship in ways that may, eventually, take us beyond those traditions. I shall spend the bulk of my time in this chapter, then, talking about ecological citizenship, but I would first like to underscore my sense of the importance of environmental, rights-based, citizenship by saying a little more about it.

## Liberal Citizenship and the Environment

The importance of rights to the contemporary citizenship idea cannot and should not be denied, and this is as true of the environmental context as of any other. Dinah Shelton distinguishes three ways in which the rights and environment contexts can come together. First, the objective of environmental protection might be pursued using existing human rights, 'such as the rights to life, personal security, health, and food... [I]n this regard, a safe and healthy environment may be viewed either as a pre-condition to the exercise of existing rights or as inextricably entwined with the enjoyment of these rights' (Shelton 1991: 105). In this context, Christopher Miller points out that:

By the time of the 1972 (Stockholm) United Nations Conference on the Human Environments the idea that an acceptable environment might constitute a precondition for the enjoyment of certain human rights no longer seemed controversial:

> Man has the fundamental right to freedom, equality and adequate conditions of life, in an environment of a quality that permits a life of dignity and well-being.

Fifteen years later and following the next conference of a similar stature, environmental quality had acquired the status of a 'fundamental' human right:

> All human beings have the fundamental right to an environment adequate for their health and well-being'         (Miller 1998: 1–2)

Second, says Shelton, the list of human rights might be extended to include the right to a liveable and sustainable environment, and third, a right *of* the environment itself might be established (Shelton 1991: 105; see also Turner 1986: 9; Waks 1996: 143).

There is much that might be said about all this. Ralf Dahrendorf wonders, for example, whether the idea of environmental rights (in Shelton's second usage above) makes sense at all: 'I am not sure whether one can stipulate an entitlement for all of us as world citizens to a liveable habitat, and thus to actions which sustain it' (Dahrendorf 1994: 18; see also Hayward 2000: 560–3; 2002: 247–52), and Leonard Waks points out that much intellectual energy could be spent adjudicating between the conflicts of priority that environmental rights claims satisfaction will bring in their train (Waks 1996: 139, 142). Similarly, when rights are enshrined in constitutions the question arises as to whether they are undemocratic, particularly in terms of their 'binding the future' (Hayward 2002: 238–41). There is also the problem of practicability: 'the nature of environmental problems is such that their causes are often difficult or impossible to identify with the degree of accuracy necessary to support legal action against specific alleged polluters' (Hayward 2000: 564). Hayward himself has suggested cutting the Gordian knot of determining the content of substantive environmental rights by focusing instead on procedural rights, such as the right to know, for example, in the context of environmental planning (Hayward 2000: 563–4; 2001: 120–1; 2002: 244–7). What seems incontrovertible is that the issues of environmental rights and citizenship are intimately linked—'something of this kind may well belong on the agenda of citizenship' (Dahrendorf 1994: 18)—and a full descriptive treatment of environmentalism and citizenship would involve devoting considerable attention to the establishing and claiming of environmental rights.

One key context for the idea of environmental rights is national constitutions, and Tim Hayward points out that 'more than 70 countries have constitutional environmental provisions of some kind, and in at least 30 cases these take the form of environmental rights... No recently promulgated constitution has omitted reference to environmental principles, and many older constitutions are being amended to include them' (Hayward 2000: 558). Constitutions might be regarded as standards by which behaviour and performance are judged, and the political importance of the presence of environmental statutes in constitutions should not be underestimated. Hayward offers a concise series of answers to his own question, 'Why adopt a constitutional approach to environmentalism?':

One major reason is that environmental problems today are such that adequate solutions to them will require large-scale cooperation within and between polities: to secure such cooperation it is necessary that there be widely agreed general principles about its basis; for such principles to be binding and legitimate within a polity they need to be set above the vicissitudes of everyday political expediency...

An advantage of pursuing environmental ends by means of constitutional rights is that in doing so one can draw normative and practical support from an established discourse of fundamental human rights...Rights mark the seriousness, the 'trumping' status, of environmental concern.          (Hayward 2001: 118–9)

For Hayward, then, constitutions provide the context for agreement on basic principles. Importantly, too, these principles are non-negotiable and have a 'trumping' quality that sets them above and apart from contingent circumstances. These are vital matters, and Hayward's brief but cogent remarks are enough to illustrate the political importance of environmental citizenship understood as the defining, enshrining, and claiming of environmental rights.

Even when not enshrined in constitutions, the vocabulary of rights has tremendous discursive and political potential. The important 'environmental justice' movement in the United States, for example, has tapped very successfully into the civil rights language of US political culture (Hofrichter 1994; Szasz 1994; Dowie 1995; Taylor 1995; Pulido 1996; Schlosberg 1999). Environmental justice activists might plausibly be regarded as 'environmental citizens', understood as claimers of the right referred to by Christopher Miller, above: 'All human beings have the fundamental right to an environment adequate for their health and well-being'. Reid and Taylor graphically and explicitly refer to such activists as 'ecological citizens', whose 'lives were fairly well contained within the dominant narratives until they became aware of environmental damage in their home, neighborhood, or beloved commons or wilds, thus rupturing the logic of their American Dream' (2000: 458). Apart from a quibble with their vocabulary—I regard environmental justice activists as 'environmental' rather than 'ecological' citizens—I endorse Reid and Taylor's view that the environmental justice movement is a form of environmental citizenship.

With half an eye on what is to come, it is also worth noting that Reid and Taylor offer a convincing *materialist* account of the source and nature of environmental citizenship. They believe, rightly in my opinion, that some people are more likely to be environmental citizens than others, and that the likelihood of environmental citizenship is in direct proportion to the lived experience of systematic exposure to environmental break-down. They begin by pointing out that:

The capacity of ecological processes—to absorb or transmute toxins, to replenish populations, to buffer dislocations in cycles, to calibrate immune systems—wears out in certain sites. It is these points of rupture in this thin green line that this article focuses on, because we see these as the world-historical points of potentially revolutionary resistance.

(Reid and Taylor 2000: 454)

More specifically they ask: 'where are the sites at which we can likely shake loose of hegemonic mists and spectres?' And they answer as follows:

The privileged site, we would argue, is in solidarity with those emergent forms of citizen politics where ordinary people are finding ways to take public action in defiance of the reproductive logos of the life-world as it is rooted for them in particular places. It is hard to know what to call this site. We variously call it "ecological citizenship" and "reproductive citizenship." It is a privileged position for clear thinking because, under existing capitalism, it is one of a decreasing number of social positions from which one cannot escape the contradictions that are reaching the explosion point.     (Reid and Taylor 2000: 455)

As examples of such social positions of ecological resistance, Reid and Taylor offer 'ecosystem' people whose livelihood depends on direct subsistence and whose lives are therefore rendered immediately precarious in the event of environmental stress, and the grassroots environmental justice activists referred to above. This materialist account of the generation of environmental citizenship contrasts vividly with the more exhortatory rhetoric of 'changes of consciousness', and I shall say more about this kind of account in the context of ecological citizenship, below.

I hope that these brief remarks are enough to indicate both the scope and the growing political importance of environmental citizenship. Having established this, though, I reiterate that it would be a mistake to assume that the rights-based view of environmental citizenship is exhaustive of the citizenship–environment relationship. I think that Peter Christoff overstates his case when he writes that: 'Ecological citizenship is *centrally* defined by its attempt to extend social welfare discourse to recognise "universal" principles relating to environmental rights and centrally incorporate these in law, culture and politics' (Christoff 1996: 161, emphasis added).

## Civic Republican Citizenship and the Environment

Before outlining the ways in which I think ecological citizenship (in contrast to environmental citizenship) 'overflows' the categories of liberal citizenship, it is worth noting that the second of the three types of citizenship described in Chapter 2, civic republican citizenship, is also of relevance in the environmental context. We noted in Chapter 2 that the idea of the 'common good' is a feature of civic republican discourse. Since environmental sustainability as a social objective is so easily translatable into 'common good' language (e.g. see B. Barry 1999: 66, and Light 2002: 166, for an explicit endorsement of an ecological republicanism for 'common good' reasons), it is not surprising to find commentators seeking intellectual resources for the idea of environmental citizenship in the civic republican tradition. This is very much the tack taken by Mark Sagoff, for example, to the point, indeed, where citizenship is *defined* by pursuit of the common good:

I shall be concerned with two rather abstract social roles we all play, namely, the role of citizen and the role of consumer. As a *citizen*, I am concerned with the public interest, rather than my own interest; with the good of the community rather than simply the well-being of my family...In my role as a *consumer*, in other words, I concern myself with personal or self-regarding wants and interests; I pursue the goals I have as an individual.                    (Sagoff 1988: 8)

It is not at all clear, of course, that citizens are only ever concerned with the public interest, but the distinction Sagoff draws—influenced by the civic republican tradition of citizenship and its virtues—offers him the opportunity to argue that sustainability will only be achieved if we act as citizens rather than as consumers.

Similarly, Patrick Curry argues explicitly for an 'ecological republicanism' on the grounds that the republican tradition is the only systematic repository of ideas relating to the common good—in this case the common good of sustainability. He defines the common good as 'both that which is needful to all for each person to live, within the existential limits of life itself a fully human life; and that which can only be generated, in effect, by all together' (2000: 1061). For Curry, the republican tradition distinguishes importantly between public duties and private virtues, and he endorses Machiavelli's view about what should happen in case of conflict between them: 'for civic republicans like Machiavelli, where there are conflicts between public duties and private virtues, the latter must give way, or else both decline together' (2000: 1061). He goes on to comment that 'In the Machiavellian view, any community which values either aggressive private enterprise or passive personal salvation more than public service is well underway to disaster' (2000: 1062).

Both Sagoff and Curry, then, regard the pursuit of the sustainable society as being about sacrificing personal inclinations or preferences to the common good. The civic republican tradition provides them with a worked-out—if subordinate, in contemporary citizenship terms—repository of ideas in this regard. All this is enough to show that both of the major citizenship traditions—liberal and civic republican—can be fruitfully connected with the 'project' of environmental sustainability. But I do not think that this project can be fully captured by these traditions, either together or in isolation. At the heart, I believe, of the tendency to overflow is the non-territorial nature of environmental sustainability as a social objective. Non-territoriality was flagged in Chapter 2 as a key feature of post-cosmopolitan citizenship, and so now I discuss the specific ecological inflection of the idea in the context of ecological citizenship.

## Ecological Non-territoriality

It has become de rigueur to point out that many environmental problems are international problems—global warming, ozone depletion, acid rain—and that they are *constitutively* international in the sense that they do not, cannot, and will never respect national boundaries in their effects. If ecological citizenship is to make any sense, then, it has to do so outside the realm of activity most normally associated with contemporary citizenship: the nation-state. As Peter Christoff points out, 'because of the nation-state's territorial boundedness, ecological citizens... increasingly work "beyond" and "around" as well as "in and against" the state' (1996: 160). This might appear to be a statement of fact, but it presupposes what this chapter hopes to confirm, namely that the political activity to which Christoff refers can be regarded as *citizenly* activity.

It is crucial to see that, as well as taking us beyond the nation-state, ecological citizenship also takes us beyond both a simple internationalism and a more complex cosmopolitanism. Ecological citizenship works with a novel conception of political space that builds in a concrete and material way on the 'historical' reasons for obligation we saw Judith Lichtenberg outlining in Chapter 2. Let me quote the key passage from that chapter:

Lichtenberg distinguishes between what she calls 'historical' and 'moral' arguments. The moral view has it that 'A owes something positive to B . . . not in virtue of any causal role he has had in B's situation or any prior relationship or agreement, but just because, for example, he is able to benefit B or alleviate his plight' (Lichtenberg 1981: 80).

In contrast, the historical view suggests that, 'what A owes to B he owes in virtue of some antecedent action, undertaking, agreement, relationship, or the like'. (Lichtenberg 1981: 81)

I characterized the 'moral' view of obligation as that of the Good Samaritan, and the 'historical' view as that of the Good Citizen. What I want to show here is that there is a specifically ecological conception of political space, and that this gives rise to the kinds of obligations that lead to citizenship rather than Samaritanism.

In this context Bart van Steenbergen distinguishes usefully between the 'world citizen' and the 'earth citizen' (van Steenbergen 1994a: 8). van Steenbergen offers the 'global businessperson' as an illustration of the world citizen:

this new global businessperson is, so to speak, 'foot-loose'. He or she has lost any specific attachment with place. As part of the jet-set he or she has literally lost contact with the earth since he or she spends much time thousands of feet above the surface of our planet. The result seems to be a de-nationalized global elite that at the same time lacks any global civic sense of responsibility.

(van Steenbergen 1994b: 149)

Richard Falk, similarly, recounts a Danish businessman's understanding of what it meant to think of himself as a 'global citizen':

It meant that he slept in the same kind of hotels whether he was in Tokyo or London or New York, that he talked English everywhere, that there was a global culture of experience, symbols and infrastructure that was supporting his way of life . . . His sense of being global went with a loss of any sense of cultural specificity that could be connected with a special attachment with place or community.

(Falk 1994: 134)

The common theme in both of these reflections is that a global reach and range does not in any way imply an ecologically responsible global reach and range: the global manager and the global capitalist have 'no particular links with the planet' (van Steenbergen 1994*b*: 150). The earth citizen possesses a sense of local and global place, while world citizens make their deracinated way around an undifferentiated globe.

Ecological citizens, then, are not merely 'international' or even 'global'—but nor are they cosmopolitan, if by this we mean that they inhabit the space created in and by the unreal conditions of the ideal-speech situation, or in virtue of their being part of a 'common humanity'. I remarked in Chapter 2 that the principal difference between cosmopolitan and post-cosmopolitan citizenship is that between the 'thin' community of common humanity and the 'thick' community of 'historical obligation'. It will also be remembered that I adapted Lichtenberg's notion to the context of globalization in which globalizing countries, and some of their citizens, have an 'always already' impact on other countries and their citizens. As a particular instantiation of post-cosmopolitan citizenship, ecological citizenship brings out this cosmopolitan/post-cosmopolitan contrast very clearly. Ecological citizenship's version of the community of historical, or always-already, obligation is best expressed via the earthy notion of the 'ecological footprint'. This, in considerable contrast to the nation-state, the international community, the globe, the world, or the metaphorical table around which cosmopolitanism's ideal speakers are sat, is ecological citizenship's version of political space. Let me say something more, then, about the ecological footprint.

Nicky Chambers, Craig Simmons, and Mathis Wackernagel point out that 'Every organism, be it a bacterium, whale or person, has an impact on the earth. We all rely upon the products and services of nature, both to supply us with raw materials and to assimilate our wastes. The impact we have on our environment is related to the "quantity" of nature that we use or "appropriate" to sustain our consumption patterns' (2000: p. xiii). Wackernagel then defines the ecological footprint as 'the land (and water) area that would be required to support a defined human population and material standard indefinitely' Wackernagel and Rees (1996: 158). It will be immediately apparent that difficulties of measurement dog the idea of the ecological footprint but without, in my opinion, undermining the basic idea it conveys. To eliminate unnecessary complications, though, allow me to adapt Wackernagel's definition by leaving out the 'indefinitely' condition. The ecological footprint then becomes a time-slice indicator of a human community's metabolistic relationship with the goods and services provided by its natural environment:

Ecological footprint analysis is an accounting tool that enables us to estimate the resource consumption and waste assimilation requirements of a defined human population or economy in terms of a corresponding productive land area. Typical questions we can ask with this tool include: how dependent is our study population on resource imports from 'elsewhere' and on the waste assimilation capacity of the global commons? (Wackernagel and Rees 1996: 9)

Chambers and her co-authors offer us a representative example of the kinds of factors that combine in calculating the size of an ecological footprint:

Consider a cooked meal of lamb and rice. The lamb requires a certain amount of grazing land, road space for transportation, and energy for processing, transportation and cooking. Similarly, the rice requires arable land for production, road space for transportation and energy for processing, transportation and cooking. A detailed ecological footprint analysis would consider all of these environmental impacts, and possibly more, when calculating a total footprint.

(Chambers *et al.* 2000: 60)

The potentially asymmetric relationship between the space actually inhabited by a given human population and the ecological space required to sustain it is graphically illustrated by Wackernagel:

[I]magine what would happen to any modern city or urban region— Vancouver, Philadelphia or London—as defined by its political global per capita 'quotas' in line with a set of 'equity principles' of sustainable development. For example, assuming a global target of 11.1 gigatonnes $CO_2$ emissions is required to maintain climate stability by 2050, and assuming that global population in 2050 is 9.8 billion, the per capita 'environmental space' for energy is 1.1 tonnes per year. UK per capita production of $CO_2$ is in the region of 9 tonnes, thus implying a reduction in UK emissions by about 85 per cent.

(Chambers *et al*. 2000: 21)

Two things should be noted in this quotation. First, there is a presumption that, absent qualifying conditions, ecological space should be divided equally among its potential recipients. Second, there is the observed fact that, in connection with $CO_2$ emissions at least, ecological space is unequally distributed. All the evidence and calculations suggest, indeed, that this inequality of distribution across a whole range of environmental goods and services is systematically tipped in favour of wealthy countries and their wealthier inhabitants (Chambers *et al*. 2000: 122–3).

Now there are various ways of disaggregating the human community so as to determine to whom or what ecological space quotas should be applied. We might think of states, regions, cities, or towns, for example. We might also think of individuals, and two issues count in favour of doing so here. First, while it may be interesting to see that 'the average Briton's' occupation of ecological space is five times larger than the sustainability objective says it ought to be, this says nothing about the distribution of ecological space among individuals *within* Britain. Second, the context of our discussion is citizenship, and if ecological citizenship is to be related to the responsibilities incurred by the over-occupation of ecological space, then these responsibilities must at some point relate to individual citizens. I am sufficiently voluntarist to agree with Marcel Wissenburg that:

'hether or not liberal democracy [or any other political form, in prin-
 le] can realize its potential for sustainability, whether or not it will

boundaries, the area of built-up land, or the concentration of socio-economic activities, if it were enclosed in a glass or plastic hemisphere that let in light but prevented material things of any kind from entering or leaving...The health and integrity of the entire human system so contained would depend entirely on whatever was initially trapped within the hemisphere. It is obvious to most people that such a city would cease to function and its inhabitants would perish within a few days. (Wackernagel and Rees 1996: 9)

In effect, Wackernagel's city borrows ecological space from somewhere else to enable it to survive. As long as ecological space is regarded as unlimited, this is an unremarkable fact. The 'ecological space debt' incurred by the city can be redeemed by drawing on the limitless fund of natural resources elsewhere in the world. But if we start thinking in terms of limits or thresholds, locally, regionally, or globally, we encounter the possibility of unredeemable ecological space debt—unredeemable because the fund on which to draw is exhausted or degraded.

Another way of thinking about this is in terms of the relationship between the occupation of ecological space and environmental sustainability. In a world of thresholds and tolerances, environmental sustainability sets limits on the amount of ecological space that can be sustainably occupied. These limits might apply either to individuals or to communities. In principle it is possible broadly to determine the amount—or quota—of ecological space available to any individual or community, consistent with the sustainability objective. Again, th' quota might apply either to a comprehensive package of en' onmental resources, or to one or some of them. Chamber' her colleagues outline the principle in the following w' they offer the example of $CO_2$ emissions:

'Environmental space' is a methodology for achieving su' it is one of the few indicator approaches that not only amounts of ecological capacity used by people, but ' that could be used in a sustainable world...Once ' space' for those key resources has been defined, be able to prevent society's developing into a global Manhattan and whether or not the sustainable liberal democratic society will offer more room for the free flowering of nature—indeed, whether any political system can do any of these things—ultimately depends on the preferences of humans. (Wissenburg 1998: 219)

This is not to underestimate the need for collective action, and nor do I subscribe to a naive voluntarism that ignores the powerful political and economic interests that structure the world in unsustainable ways. Ecological citizens will avail themselves of the opportunities for collective action with which political systems present them. Obviously these political systems and the parts that comprise them (states, corporations, councils, and so on) are also producers of ecological footprints, and if they are implicated in or endorse unsustainable practices they should be held to account. But it is a moot point whether these political formations can be talked of as 'citizens'. For the purposes of this book I assume that they cannot, but they are made up of individuals whose attempts to push them in a sustainability direction can be regarded as citizenly. Goodall has written that 'it will require many individual acts, at the local level, in order to bring about significant change. If every individual were to buy ozone-friendly products, burn less fuel and join recycling schemes then producers would have to change' (Goodall 1994: 7). I regard these as acts of citizenship—but they will also inevitably bring individuals into conflict with political and economic structures whose intentions are profoundly unsustainable, and at this point ecological citizenship will demand collective as well as individual action. Hence the focus on individuals—but on the understanding that these individuals will be operating in the interstices of social life.

Before going any further, let me outline a difficulty with the ecological footprint idea and try to respond to it. On the face of it the idea trades on a notion that will already be regarded as discredited by many people: limits to growth. Ever since Donella Meadows and her Club of Rome colleagues announced in

*The Limits to Growth* (1974) that infinite growth in a finite system is impossible, critics have been quick to point out flaws in the argument. Such critics have referred, variously, to poor modelling of the 'world system' on which the report's conclusions were based, to the recent historical record that suggests that predictions of resource depletion were wide of the mark; and to the report's underestimation of the capacity for human ingenuity and technology to get more from less.

A range of responses to these criticisms might be made, some simple, some more complex. I harbour a smidgin of sympathy for the most simple of all, which is to ask 'how much nature do we have as compared with how much nature we use?' (Chambers *et al.* 2000: 29). The only context in which this question makes no sense at all (as fundamentalist critics of the limits to growth thesis would have us believe) is that of a totally cornucopian world in which infinite substitutability of resources is possible. And in contexts in which the question makes at least *some* sense (i.e. all reasonably imaginable contexts), the idea of ecological space and its distributive implications seems necessarily to arise.

A slightly more complex version of the same response is to recognize that it is indeed not so much a question of when the atmospheric tolerance for $CO_2$ will 'run out', as it were, but that increased concentrations have unpredictable effects on the climate which disproportionately affect those most vulnerable to them. While it might be debatable whether we could ever arrive at a definitive figure for fair per capita $CO_2$ emission, in other words, we can be fairly certain that the planet's temperature is rising for anthropogenic reasons, that some people contribute more to this phenomenon than others, and that some people suffer more from the unpredictability this brings in its train than others.

From the point of view of the idea of ecological citizenship, it does not matter which of these responses we choose. Whether the footprint is specific, calculable, and inscribed in a limits to growth framework, or whether it is regarded merely as an expression of the unavoidable impact every individual has on the environment in the production and reproduction of human life, the footprint gives rise to the 'always already' community of obligation that I have adapted from Judith Lichtenberg.

Another way of putting this is to say that the idea of the ecological footprint converts relationships we had thought to be 'Samaritan' into relationships of citizenship. And it does so not by some sleight of hand, but by pointing to 'antecedent actions and relationships' (in Lichtenberg's terms) where we had thought they did not exist. These actions and relationships give rise to the kinds of obligations that it is more appropriate to regard as obligations of citizenship than of Samaritanism. A key feature of this is to see that the 'space' of ecological citizenship cannot be understood in terms of contiguous territory. The effects that give rise to ecological citizenship are best captured in terms of 'action at a distance'. The contiguous territorial metaphors that are common to both liberal and civic republican citizenship are unhelpful here. Even cosmopolitan citizenship shares the idea of contiguous territory in the guise of 'one world'. In contrast, the key ecological citizenship point is that 'the footprint is not usually a continuous piece of land or land of one particular type or quality. The globalization of trade has increased the likelihood that the bioproductive areas required to support the consumption—of the richer countries at least—are scattered all over the planet' (Chambers *et al.* 2000: 60). More pithily, Wackernagel writes that: 'Bits of a population's Ecological Footprint can be all over the world' (Wackernagel and Rees 1996: 53). In sum, ecological citizenship's 'community' corresponds to Curry's 'minimal definition': '(1) a social connection such that members impact upon each other in ways that affect their material or embodied behavior; and ... (2) an experiential correction to the others involved: an awareness of other members of the community'. Crucially, says Curry, 'These two requirements mean that community will very often entail a shared geographical space, but does not absolutely require it' (2000: 1060).

The 'space' of ecological citizenship is therefore not something *given* by the boundaries of nation-states or of supranational organizations such as the European Union, or even by the imagined territory of the cosmopolis. It is, rather, *produced* by the metabolistic and material relationship of individual people with their environment. This relationship gives rise to an ecological footprint which gives rise, in turn, to relationships with those on whom it impacts. We are unlikely to have met, or be ever likely to meet, those with whom we have these relationships. They may live near by or be far away, and they may be of this generation or of generations yet to be born. It is important to recognize too, of course, that they may live in our own nation-state. In this last case, though, I do not have ecological citizenly relations with them because they are fellow-citizens in the traditional nation-state sense, but because they (may) inhabit the territory created by my ecological footprint. By definition, then, ecological citizenship is a citizenship of strangers—as is, in a sense, all citizenship: 'citizens accept that in principle and in fact they are and will remain strangers to each other: there are more citizens in any nation-state than any individual could meet, let alone get to know well, in a lifetime' (Roche 1987: 376). (Attempts to find a better metaphorical representation than 'strangers' of the fundamental identity of citizenship nearly always return to it in the end. Iseult Honohan's stretching of the 'colleague' metaphor to the point where her colleagues no longer know each other—thereby becoming strangers—is a case in point; Honohan 2001: 58.) The additional point of ecological citizenship, however, is that we are strangers not only to each other, but to each other's place, and even time. The obligations of the ecological citizen extend through time as well as space, towards generations yet to be born. Ecological citizens know that today's acts will have implications for tomorrow's people, and will argue that 'generationism' is akin to, and as indefensible as, racism or sexism. They will unequivocally endorse Maurice Roche's view that:

[T]he dominant paradigm of social citizenship, including Marshall's version of it, rests on unspoken and usually barely recognized temporal assumptions. It tends to take it for granted that the only issues worth considering are those connected with the social rights and welfare needs of the contemporary set of generations...Nothing reveals the outdated character of the dominant paradigm more than this.

(Roche 1992: 242)

This account of the *production* of political space (Behnke 1997) and the citizen responsibilities to which it gives rise contrasts vividly with another more common way of generating ethical duties in the political–ecological context. In this connection, many so-called deep ecologists argue for a different understanding of our relationship with the rest of the non-human natural world. We might call this an 'ontological' approach to the problem of the definition of the community of ecological citizenship. Deep ecologists (of a certain type, cf. Dobson 2000a: 46–51) suggest that our pre-political relationship with the non-human natural world is best understood in terms of embeddedness and codependence rather than differentiation and dominance. This ontology of embeddedness is said to give rise to a duty of care more readily than does an ontology of differentiation. As Warwick Fox, a leading exponent of this view, has written:

For example, when asked why he does not plough the ground, the Nez Percé American Indian Smohalla does not reply with a closely reasoned explanation as to why the ground has intrinsic value but rather with a rhetorical question expressive of a deep identification with the earth: 'Shall 1 take a knife and tear my mother's breast?'

(Fox 1986: 76)

Once the ontological shift has taken place, the question is not 'what reasons do I have for caring for the non-human natural world?', but 'what reasons can there possibly be for not caring for it?'. The ontology of embeddedness makes wanton destruction of the environment look as odd as wanton destruction of the self.

Another account of ecological citizenship in a similar vein comes from Reid and Taylor—an account which makes it clear that the perceived strength of the ontological approach to the community of ecological citizenship is in fact its most profound weakness. Reid and Taylor write that 'We are calling for a return to Merleau-Ponty's understanding of the "flesh of the world" as a way to think the simultaneity of Being as bodily, ecological, historical, ethical, cultural, and political' (Reid and Taylor 2000: 452). This is another way of expressing the ontology of embeddedness to which I referred in the previous paragraph. On this account, our modes of being are not separate but connected, and at a pre-reflective level they coexist simultaneously even if our post-reflective accounts of them take a 'serial' form. Reid and Taylor believe that this ontology gives rise to a rather specific understanding of the community of citizenship:

At the heart of our concerns is the question of citizenship. What does it mean to talk of ecological citizenship? Can Merleau-Ponty's notion of the 'flesh of the world' take us beyond a citizenship based in decontextualized abstractions of 'natural rights' to concepts of citizenship that recognize that we are dwellers on the land, that make us, once again, natives of the Earth? (Reid and Taylor 2000: 452)

Reid and Taylor suggest that the strength of this account of the citizenship community is that it does not deal in the currency of 'decontextualized abstraction'. This is indeed an admirable objective, but while the idea of the 'flesh of the world' toys with a materialist account of community, its roots remain in the idealist tradition, depending, as it does, on a *change of consciousness* for its effect. Put differently, the idea of 'the flesh of the world' is itself a decontextualized abstraction—as much of one, indeed, as the ideal speech community on which so much cosmopolitanism depends.

My overall sense, therefore, is that to try to generate the community of ecological citizenship deductively from first principles is a mistake. Curry, in an article to which I have already referred, gets into something of a tangle trying to do so. It will be remembered that in working up his idea of ecological republicanism he posits two requirements for a 'minimal definition of human community'. They are: '(1) a social connection such that members impact upon each other in ways that affect their material or embodied behavior; and...(2) an experiential correction to the others involved: an awareness of other members of the community' (2000: 1060). He wants his ecological republicanism to embrace a wider community than the human one, though, so his question is whether the idea of an ecological community is consistent with these two conditions. The first condition, he says, is consistent with his wish to extend the community beyond human beings, but 'The second requirement...seems considerably more problematic. To begin with, we must admit that short of pantheism (or rather panpsychism), the abiotic "members" of an ecological community can have no awareness as it is usually thought of. This is actually a grave concession, since it appears that sentient beings alone qualify for such membership' (2000: 1064).

The stumbling block for Curry's human and non-human community of ecological republicans, then, is that (some of) its non-human members are not aware of each other in the required way. Instead of rethinking his deductive approach to defining the ecological citizenship community as I would counsel him to do, though, Curry simply reaffirms his determination to include anything and everything in it:

let us hypothesize that anything called an ecological community should indeed include and respect the experience of the organisms concerned—including, but not limited to, humans—of integral elements of what we could defensibly call their community, however tacit and inarticulate that awareness might be.

(Curry 2000: 1065)

Unsurprisingly, Curry's self-imposed definitional problem pops up again: 'It remains true that this understanding still cannot bring the nonliving elements of ecosystems into line with my second proposed criterion' (2000: 1066). At which point Curry rather unsatisfactorily solves his second criterion problem by simply dropping it: 'But those who think this failure (if such it is) withholds the status of community from ecosystems should first ask themselves, is a biotic community possible, or even imaginable, without its abiotic elements? The answer is clearly, no' (2000: 1066).

The citizenship communities offered to us by cosmopolitanism, by Reid and Taylor, and by Curry, might all appear rather different, then, but they have something crucially important in common. They are all deduced from first principles rather than induced from the material and differentiated conditions of the reproduction of daily life. Cosmopolitanism's community is deduced from the preconditions of the ideal speech community; Reid and Taylor's community is deduced from an ontological shift that contains the very notion of community it posits; and Curry assumes that the community whose existence he is trying to prove can be deduced from an all-embracing set of criteria for defining 'community', one of which he then drops.

In contrast, the community of ecological citizenship is created by the material activities of human beings themselves. Ecological citizenship rejects the idealist view that 'we belong morally to one world community of human beings' (Dower 2002: 146), or that the key point is the contested ontological one that we are somehow 'both part of as well as apart from the order of nature' (Barry 2002: 144). The material approach to defining the community of ecological citizenship has the advantage of not having to operate in the realm of meta-argument. The citizenship community envisaged by cosmopolitans, for example, relies on us having accepted the communicative rules of engagement and the subsequent 'fact' of the ideal speech situation, for example. This is a contentious rather than a settled matter, and so any notion of citizenship erected on the foundations of these assumptions will be prone not only to its own insecurities, but to those of these assumptions too: 'nonsense on stilts', as Jeremy Bentham would have it. Similarly, the ontological shift proposed by Reid and Taylor is contested at all levels. Cartesian-type binary ripostes to homogenizing 'flesh of the world' ontologies are alive and kicking, and so erecting a contested notion of citizenship on foundations that are themselves contested seems ill-advised. The only foundational thought that my post-cosmopolitan understanding of ecological citizenship demands we accept, in contrast, is that human beings make an impact on the environment as they go about the production and repro-duction of their daily lives. This seems less contentious as a means of getting the community of ecological citizenship off the ground than either the ideal speech situation or a grandiose ontological shift.

This may be the best place to put down another marker: I regard ecological citizenship as a fundamentally anthropocen-tric notion. This is to say that while ecological citizenship obvi-ously has to do with the relationship between human beings and the non-human natural world as well as between human beings themselves, there is no need—either politically or intel-lectually—to express this relationship in ecocentric terms. Let me try to make this clearer by commenting on a remark made by Fred Steward. He writes as follows:

The politics of citizenship runs into a second major problem in its encounter with environmentalism. The concept is formulated to deal with the relationship between the individual and the community within human society, but the fundamental issue addressed by green politics is the status of nature as separate and distinct from human society. Does nature have *rights* and if so, then how are they to be articulated and represented in a discourse of social citizenship?

(Steward 1991: 73)

The implicit attempt to generate a notion of environmental or ecological citizenship by referring to the 'rights of nature' obviously runs into the 'nonsense on stilts' difficulties referred to above. For those who believe that nature has *no* rights, any idea of ecological citizenship that depends on the rights of nature will fall at the first hurdle. One argument for making ecological citizenship an anthropocentric idea, then, is expedience.

But there is another, more principled argument, one drawn from what we might call 'future generationism'. Its most articulate exponent, Bryan Norton, has written that:

> introducing the idea that other species have intrinsic value, that humans should be 'fair' to all other species, provides no operationally recognizable constraints on human behaviour that are not already implicit in the generalized, cross-temporal obligations to protect a healthy, complex, and autonomously functioning system for the benefit of future generations of humans.          (Norton 1991: 239)

Norton's basic idea is that the vast majority of environmentalists' demands regarding the protection of non-human nature can be met through attending to our obligations to future generations of human beings. These obligations, he says, amount to passing on a 'healthy, complex and autonomously functioning system', and so the sustaining of such a system is a by-product, as it were, of doing the right thing by future human beings. From this point of view there is no need for arcane, contentious, and politically unpopular debates regarding either 'the rights of nature' or the 'ontological shift' favoured by deep ecologists. It is enough to recognize that we have obligations to future humans, and that these obligations include that of providing them with the means to life (broadly understood—I shall be more precise shortly). As I pointed out above, the ecological footprint extends into the future as well as across territories in the present, so the obligations of which Norton speaks can properly be thought of in terms of citizenship. So I regard ecological citizenship as anthropocentric, but anthropocentric in a 'long-sighted' way (Barry 1999: 223). John Barry rightly points out that:

ecological stewardship [which Barry equates with ecological citizenship; see 2002: 146] 'taps into' and incorporates the idea that one of the most politically and ethically robust grounds upon which to defend the preservation of nature, and many other policy objectives of environmental politics, is an appeal to the obligations we owe to future generations ... this idea of obligations to future generations is integral to the stewardship ethic. (Barry 2002: 142)

A familiar injunction in this regard is offered by Mark Smith: 'present generations should not act in ways which jeopardize the existence of future generations and their ability to live in dignity, and, if we do act in ways which contain the possibility of adverse future consequences, we should minimize such risks' (1998: 97).

For all its superficial radical attractions, then, I do not endorse explicitly ecocentric accounts of ecological citizenship. The most fundamental reason I have for rejecting ecocentric ecological citizenship is that I regard the principal virtue of ecological citizenship to be that of justice, and I believe that justice can only very arguably be predicated of non-human natural beings. Put differently, the community of justice is, for me, a human community, so if the community of ecological citizens is primarily a community of justice, the community must be a human one. While there is considerable metaphorical mileage in the idea that 'Citizenship, in its fullest expression, must be understood as encompassing the more-than-human community' (Curtin 2002: 302), my view is that we can only have moral as opposed to citizenly relations with non-human beings. I shall say more about justice as the principal virtue of ecological citizenship in a subsequent section.

Put differently again, we need to distinguish between the moral community and the community of citizens—a difference that tracks the distinction I have drawn before between the Good Samaritan and the Good Citizen. I believe that the moral community can be usefully regarded in an ecocentric way, but the community of citizens cannot. In this connection, I think that Mark Smith gets the two communities mixed up in the following reflection: 'Ecological citizenship... transforms the nature of the moral community itself, by displacing the human species from the central ethical position it has always held' (1998: 99). To my mind it is not ecological *citizenship* that transforms the moral community, but environmental *philosophy*, and particularly environmental *ethics*. Ecological citizenship transforms the community of citizenship, not the moral community. In sum I endorse Robin Attfield's view that 'the boundaries of moral concern, including the concern of global citizens, do not and should not exclude non-human interests, even though global citizenship is almost entirely confined to human beings' (Attfield 2002: 197). I similarly endorse Andrew Light's definition of ecological citizenship as 'the description of some set of moral and political rights and responsibilities of agents in a democratic community, defined in terms of their obligations to other humans taking into account those forms of human engagement and interaction that best preserve the long-term sustainability of nature' (2002: 159). As Light correctly points out, in echo of Attfield, 'Such a view need not consider nature as a direct object of moral concern or as a moral subject in its own right' (2002: 159).

Returning to a point made earlier, one signal contrast between cosmopolitan and post-cosmopolitan citizenship is that for the former the existence of the community of citizenship is simply *announced*, whereas for the latter it is *produced*. In the more specific context of this chapter, I have argued for the produced nature of the community of ecological citizenship via the metabolistic idea of the ecological footprint. In describing post-cosmopolitan citizenship in Chapter 2, I also pointed out that 'While this is a citizenship with international and intergenerational dimensions, its responsibilities are asymmetrical. Its obligations fall on those, precisely, with the capacity to "always already" act on others'. As a particular instantiation of post-cosmopolitan citizenship we would expect ecological citizenship to share these characteristics, and indeed it does. I suggested earlier that the ecological footprint gives rise to relationships with those *on whom it impacts*. Everything we have said about the differential size of ecological footprints suggests that these impacts will be asymmetrical. The relevant cleavage is that between 'globalizing' and 'globalized' individuals, where the former is taken to refer to those whose action can 'impact at a distance', and the latter to those whose actions cannot. I do not think, then, that 'Citizenship of planet earth ... embodies a new sense of the universal political subject' (Steward 1991: 74), if by this we mean citizens with reciprocal and symmetrical rights and obligations. This symmetry and reciprocity is much more a feature of cosmopolitan than of post-cosmopolitan citizenship, and Steward is speaking entirely in the cosmopolitan idiom here. As such, I think he misses what is interesting in ecological citizenship. Similarly it is not enough to say that 'Individual citizens ... owe a duty of care to the planet in terms of minimising resource consumption and pollution' (Steward 1991: 75), without specifying more carefully just *which* citizens have this duty of care. People who occupy less than their quota of ecological space have no such duty, except as a general injunction against wanton harm. The ecological footprint is key here. It is both an expression of the space of ecological citizenship and a way of framing decisions as to the direction of citizenship responsibilities. Bearing this framework in mind, we must surely resist David Miller's view that the Greenpeace activist cannot be regarded as a citizen (2002: 90). Miller offers two reasons for his conclusion: 'There is no determinate community with which she identifies politically, and no one, except perhaps other members of her groups with whom she stands in relations of reciprocity' (2002: 90). For ecological citizenship, though, the relevant political community is that created by the ecological footprint, and the footprint creates obligations that are explicitly non-reciprocal, but no less citizenly for all that.

One thing that ecological and cosmopolitan citizenship share, though, is a common lack of interest in membership as a citizenship issue. This might be regarded as curious, given that much of the recent interest in citizenship is due to the complex and plural nature of modern societies, and the consequent conundrums as far as entitlements are concerned. If entitlements are due only to citizens, then the criteria for citizenship are clearly of crucial importance. Both ecological and cosmopolitan citizenship swim against the tide here, though, and there are two reasons for this. First, the importance of the membership issue for traditional notions of citizenship is due to the tight relationship between membership and entitlement: no membership, no entitlement. Ecological citizenship's focus on duties rather than entitlements, on the other hand, makes for a much less specific relationship between the citizen and what s/he ought to do *as* a citizen. The duties of ecological citizenship are owed non-specifically. I shall say more about this in a subsequent section.

Second, the *relations* of citizenship according to the ecological conception differ from those envisaged in the traditional entitlements model. According to this latter model, the principal relationship is that between the individual citizen and the constituted political authority: the individual citizen claims entitlements from and against the constituted political authority. Ecological citizenship, in contrast, is about the horizontal relationship between citizens rather than the vertical (even if reciprocal) relationship between citizen and state. This is true of cosmopolitan citizenship too. To this extent, the importance of membership of the nation-state is downplayed, and the Rousseauian idea that the individual–state relationship is the most important one is rejected.

Ecological and cosmopolitan citizenship are therefore part of a wider recognition that 'national' citizenship needs to be supplemented by non-national features:

The period in which it was possible to conceive of citizenship in general and social citizenship in particular in national and welfare-state terms is clearly coming to an end. New positive myths and ideals of citizenship rights are developing, such as those involving notions of 'the Earth's rights', the 'rights of the unborn' and 'world citizenship'. They both enrich and complicate the more conventional modern myths and ideals relating to citizenship, such as those involving notions of human equality, of place and territorial identity, of nation and of heritage.

(Roche 1992: 244)

These references to 'world citizenship' and 'Earth's rights', though, prompt the reminder that ecological citizenship, as I understand it, differs markedly both from cosmopolitan citizenship and from some other articulations of ecological citizenship. The main differences are that in post-cosmopolitan and (my) ecological citizenship the community of citizenship is materially produced rather than pre-politically given, and that the space it inhabits is of no predetermined size: 'although the ideas about citizenship and rights have been grounded in the notion of the modern nation-state, there is no intrinsic necessity that this be so: the public sphere might be "smaller" or "larger" than the state, or may even be different' (Jelin 2000: 53).

I mentioned, above, that one of the reasons why ecological citizenship is not much concerned with the otherwise crucial issue of membership of the citizen body is that it focuses on the duties rather than the rights of citizenship. This is the subject of the following section.

## Duty and Responsibility in Ecological Citizenship

I endorse Bart van Steenbergen's view that 'There is one important difference between the environmental movement and other emancipation movements. This difference has to do with the notion of *responsibility* . . . citizenship not only concerns rights and entitlements, but also duties, obligations and responsibilities' (1994*b*: 146). A number of commentators on ecological citizenship agree with this (see e.g. Smith 1998: 99–100; Barry 1996: 126), but such a bare statement prompts two obvious yet important questions: just what are these duties, obligations, and responsibilities, and to whom or what are they owed? It also prompts a third, rather less obvious question, but one that is important as far as 'citizenship' as an idea is concerned. Whatever these duties, obligations, and responsibilities are, and to whomever or whatever they are owed, can they be regarded as obligations of citizenship, properly speaking? Finally, it will be remembered that I argued in Chapter 2 that, although the distinction between a citizenship of rights and citizenship of obligation is an important, time-honoured, and respectable way of distinguishing between liberal and civic republican citizenship, the distinction can obscure an underlying similarity between them. The similarity is that both liberal and civic republican citizenship regard rights and obligations, and the relationship between the citizen and the polity more generally, in contractual and reciprocal terms. My suggestion was that post-cosmopolitan citizenship, in contrast, takes an explicitly non-contractual view of obligation, and we would expect ecological citizenship, as an exemplar of post-cosmopolitan citizenship, to do the same. I shall deal with each of these four issues in what follows.

First, then, what are the obligations of ecological citizenship? These follow very obviously from the discussion of ecological non-territoriality in the previous section. There I argued that the 'space' of ecological citizenship is the ecological footprint, and that the ecological footprints of some members of some countries have a damaging impact on the life chances of some members of other countries, as well as members of their own country. Simply put, then, the principal ecological citizenship obligation is to ensure that ecological footprints make a sustainable, rather than an unsustainable, impact. Exactly what this means in terms of individuals' daily lives is not something that can be discussed here, and I do not propose to outline a manifesto for 'green living'. To ask for such a manifesto, indeed, is to miss a key feature of the general ecological citizenship injunction. The obligation is evidently radically indeterminate. Just what do we mean by a 'sustainable impact'? I shall spend time in Chapter 4 discussing this question in much more detail, but the key thing now is to see that the question has normative dimensions that are not susceptible to determinate answers. This does not make ecological citizenship meaningless, in the same way that recognizing that 'democracy' or 'justice' or 'freedom' have various meanings neither makes discussion of them otiose, nor instantiation of them impossible. It does mean, though, that attempts to encourage ecological citizenship, through education for example, should explicitly recognize its normative dimension. This is the subject of Chapter 5. At the most general level, and with apologies to the Brundtland Commission whose definition of sustainable development has become the most widely cited, and which I adapt somewhat for present purposes, the ecological citizen will want to ensure that her or his ecological footprint does not compromise or foreclose the ability of others in present and future generations to pursue options important to them (World Commission on Environment and Development 1987: 43).

This formulation also offers an answer to the second question: to whom or to what are the obligations of ecological citizenship owed? Once again the answer flows from the 'ecological non-territoriality' of the previous section. Ecological footprints are an expression of the impact of the production and reproduction of individuals' and collectives' daily lives on strangers near and far. It is these strangers to whom the obligations of ecological citizenship are owed. Working out the exact extent of these obligations is not something that can be done here since there are many variables to consider (which individual? which collection of individuals? which category of consumption/ production? what kind of impact—resource or waste? And so on). Chapter 3 of Wackernagel and Rees's *Our Ecological Footprint* is a good place to begin the journey of calculation. Whatever the specifics, this view of obligation contrasts with both the liberal and civic republican positions in which the scope of obligation is determined by the territorial boundaries of the polity—usually the state. Obligations might be owed either to fellow citizens or to the state itself, but even in the former case the obligations of citizenship extend no further than those who are defined as citizens by the constituted political authority in question. Obligations of ecological citizenship, on the other hand, are due to anyone who is owed ecological space. Such people might inhabit the same politically constituted space, but they might not. Just as environmental problems cross political boundaries, so do the obligations of ecological citizenship.

But they do not cross them in the same way as they do for cosmopolitan citizens. In the world of cosmopolitan citizenship, obligations—and above all the obligation to acknowledge the force of the better argument—are owed by everyone to everyone. By contrast, the obligations of ecological citizenship are owed asymmetrically. Only those who occupy ecological space in such a way as to compromise or foreclose the ability of others in present and future generations to pursue options important to them owe obligations of ecological citizenship. This last formulation also reminds us that our discussion of the ecological footprint suggested that its impact is felt in the future as well as in the present. This, then, is another way in which the ecological answer to the 'to whom?' question of citizenship obligations differs from liberal, civic republican, and cosmopolitan citizenships: such obligations are owed to the future as well as in the present. A critical implication of these types of obligation and to whom they are owed is that they contain no explicit expectations of reciprocity. If my ecological footprint is an unsustainable size, then my obligation is to reduce it. It would be absurd to ask someone in ecological space deficit reciprocally to reduce theirs. The duty to reduce the size of an overlarge footprint is, however, driven by the correlative right to sufficient ecological space.

It would be a mistake to think that the non-reciprocal nature of the ecological citizen's obligations somehow makes them open-ended. In an important criticism of an earlier version of the arguments I am making here, (Dobson 2000*b*) John Barry writes that:

While this nonreciprocal sense of compassion is doubtless commendable, Dobson's ecological citizens are more akin to ecological angels in their selfless concern for future generations, the nonhuman world, and strangers in other parts of the world. Dobson's notion of ecological citizenship demands too much, especially in the absence of any discussion of the balance to be struck between legitimate 'self-interest' and concern for others. (Barry 2002: 145–6)

My current formulation should make it clear that, while the obligations of ecological citizens have a non-reciprocal and asymmetrical character, they are not unlimited. They are owed because of an unjust distribution of ecological space, and they end when that imbalance has been addressed. I ought to point out, in any case, that despite Barry's absolutely appropriate requirement that limits be set on the ecological citizen's obligations, he does not offer any account himself of what these might be. His own formulations are as open-ended as those he criticizes: 'Rather than the individual being concerned with her own interests, she is encouraged to consider the interests of all those potentially affected by human actions' (Barry 2002: 146), and, 'we recognize that we are, to a greater or lesser extent, each other's keeper, as well as being responsible for the non-human world' (Barry 2002: 147).

This is an ironic outcome for such a self-consciously hard-headed yet ultimately soft-centred approach to ecological citizenship. The hard-headed dimension looks like this:

Advocating such a nonreciprocal notion of care for the natural world, divorced from any sense of the need and legitimacy of humans to use, consume, kill, eat, transform, and develop parts of it, is a serious flaw in Dobson's otherwise powerful idea of ecological citizenship. The advantage of casting the greening of citizenship as ecological steward-ship in this respect is that the relationship it posits between humans and nature is partial, interested, reciprocal, and ultimately based on the 'reality of the human situation' in having to interact with nature as phenomenal rather than noumenal beings.     (Barry 2002: 146)

The soft centre runs as follows:

My suggestion is that ecological stewardship traces and is related to those webs of dependence and vulnerability, those relations among people, planet, and the two together, creating a community of depend-ence and vulnerability, the most appropriate attitude toward which is a disposition of responsibility, care, and mindfulness.

(Barry 2002: 146)

I hope it is clear from everything I have said in this chapter that I am much more in sympathy with the sentiment of the first of these quotations than with those of the second. The very idea of the ecological footprint is premised on the fact that humans transform their environment in order to produce and rep-roduce their daily lives. In this sense the 'reality of the human situation' lies at the heart of my notion of ecological citizenship. Second, I do not believe this citizenship to be created, in the first instance, by 'webs of dependence and vulnerability'. What count, in contrast, are systematic relations of ecological injus-tice, of which webs of vulnerability are a symptom rather than a cause—and not all vulnerabilities can be expressed in terms of injustice (are battery hens subject to 'injustice'?). All this ought also to help answer the motivational question implicit in Barry's legitimate worry that 'Dobson does not specify the reasons why ecological citizens care; rather it is assumed that by definition they care' (2002: 146). Ecological citizens care because they want to do justice—although of course the question of why on earth they might want to do justice is one that has taxed better minds than my own.

In Chapter 2 I referred to the distinction drawn by Judith Lichtenberg between 'moral' and 'historical' obligation, and argued that the latter can be regarded as a source of obligation of a citizenship type. Non-reciprocity is a common feature of both these kinds of obligation. Given the centrality of reciprocity to theories of citizenship, though, a question for us is whether the unreciprocated and asymmetrical obligations of ecological citizenship can be regarded as citizenship obligations at all. In Chapter 2, we saw John Horton answering this question in the negative: 'The reason why reciprocal/contractual models of citizenship are attractive is precisely because they try to explain how the rights (and duties) of citizenship are circumscribed to citizens. The point about citizenship relations is that they only hold between citizens, and not, for example, between parents and children or peoples of one state and another' (Horton 1998: personal communication). I agree entirely that we need to distinguish between the moral community and the community of citizens, but not that the best way of doing so is by determining who is actually or potentially capable of making contracts or responding to prompts of reciprocity.

Horton's point is nevertheless a vital one because the moral community and the community of citizens are often confounded in commentaries on ecological citizenship. A representative example is this from Patrick Curry:

Given that those who are candidates for non-contractual duties include children, the senile, the temporarily and the permanently insane, defectives, embryos, human and otherwise, sentient animals, non-sentient animals, plants, artefacts, including art, inanimate objects, groups of all kinds, ecosystems, landscapes and places, countries, the biosphere and oneself...It follows that 'Duties need not be quasi-contractual relations between symmetrical pairs of rational human agents...To speak of duties to things in the inanimate and comprehensive sectors of my list is not necessarily to personify them superstitiously... It expresses merely that there are suitable and unsuitable ways of behaving in given situations' (Midgley 1995: 97). In other words... relieved of the 'Reciprocity Assumption', the way is clear to realise, as Sylvan and Bennett (1994) argue, that 'the ecological community forms the ethical community'.     (Curry 2000: 1067)

It is relatively uncontroversial to argue that 'duties need not be quasi-contractual relations between symmetrical pairs of rational human agents', but it is by no means certain that these duties will necessarily be of a type that we can associate with citizenship. Curry does not explicitly say here that they are, either, but this passage is part of an argument for 'ecological republicanism', some of which involves entertaining a much-expanded notion of the community of citizens. Curry's point is that we can get to such a notion only if we abandon reciprocity and contract as defining features of citizenship relations. But then he goes too far. The 'list of candidates for non-contractual duties' is a very extensive one, and Curry implicitly makes this extensive list coterminous with membership of the community of citizens. Such a move falls foul of Horton's stricture that we must have some way of distinguishing between different types of relationship, and in particular between relationships of citizenship and other sorts.

Richard Falk makes a similar mistake of elision, I believe, when he writes that,

This spirit of global citizenship is almost completely deterritorialized, and is associated with the human condition. It is not a matter of being a loyal participant who belongs to a particular political community, whether city or state, but feeling, thinking and acting for the sake of the human species, and above all for those most vulnerable and disadvantaged. As such, an African baby is an appropriate and powerful symbol of the vulnerability and solidarity of the species as a whole.

(Falk 1994: 133)

Falk rightly contrasts global citizenship with loyalty to a 'particular political community', but erroneously jumps to the conclusion that 'thinking and acting for the sake of the human species' is an expression of citizenship. The contrast between the Good Samaritan and the Good Citizen should be sufficiently firmly planted in our minds now to see that a generalized concern for the human species is more accurately expressed in terms of the former than the latter. Even Falk's more specific reference to 'the most vulnerable and disadvantaged' members of the human species does not necessarily take us into the realms of citizenship. We might have a *moral* commitment to help the global vulnerable and disadvantaged simply because we can 'alleviate their plight' (Lichtenberg 1981: 80), but this only turns into a commitment of *citizenship* if we can show that we have played a 'causal role' (Lichtenberg 1981: 80) in their situation. Symbolism, as in the case of the African baby to whom Falk refers, is entirely irrelevant to determining the community of citizens. What counts is actual, practical, material, causal relationship. This approach steers an appropriate course, I believe, between the reciprocity condition for citizenship, which is too demanding, and Falk's and Curry's indiscriminate confounding of the moral community with the community of citizens, which is too loose.

As well as being an alternative to either of these positions, it also contrasts with what we might call the 'incipient institutions' approach to making sense of non-national citizenship. It has sometimes been argued that non-national citizenship makes no sense because there is no relevant political entity within which and through which 'citizens' can claim citizenship rights and discharge citizenship obligations. There is, in other words, no world state. Supporters of the idea of global citizenship, though, will point to incipient regional and global political entities such as the European Union and the United Nations through which the idea of transnational citizenship can be exercised. They may also refer to major transnational activist organizations as prefigurative forms of a global civil society in which world citizens operate. Richard Falk, for example, writes that:

Amnesty International and Greenpeace are emblematic of this transnational militancy with an identity, itself evolving and being self-transformed, that cannot really be tied very specifically to any one country or even any region...These networks of transnational activity conceived both as a project and as a preliminary reality are producing a new orientation towards political identity and community that cumulatively can be described as global civil society.

(Falk 1994: 138)

Peter Christoff is less enthusiastic, though:

it is apparent that at present the notion of post-national ecological citizenship—the idea of becoming a 'citizen of Planet Earth'—is still largely metaphorical, despite the growing influence of environmentalists at the local, national and international levels on government policies, the evolution of transnational environmental organisations, and the growing number of international conventions and treaties.

(Christoff 1996: 163)

Certainly in contrast with the significance of national notions of citizenship, post-national conceptions are far less influential. Nevertheless, there seems to be something in all these responses to the criticism that there is no institutional evidence for, or instantiation of, transnational citizenship. The European Union, for example, is indeed a growing repository of claims and obligations of a citizenship type. The United Nations has no such competences, of course, but it might profitably be regarded as a potential agency for meeting the kinds of obligations I have associated with post-cosmopolitan citizenship. Transnational campaigning organizations such as Greenpeace might be seen in a similar light, but also as agencies whose activity crucially consists in bringing to light the 'always already' effect that globalizing nations have on those whose remit is only local. This is indeed the most profound sense in which they are prefigurative of the 'global civil society' of which Falk speaks.

However we rate the 'incipient institutions' response to the claim that there is no evidence of a transnational citizenship (and for more discussion of this issue see Dower and Williams 2002: 65–124), its gambit is to meet that claim head on. Critics of transnational citizenship say that there is no institutional evidence for it; supporters of it say that there is. The approach I have taken here is different from this. I have sought to show how the patterns and effects of globalization have given rise to a series of material conditions within which the idea of transnational citizenship obligations can make sense.

I began this section with four issues for discussion. First, what are the obligations of ecological citizenship? Second, can these obligations be regarded as ones of citizenship, properly speaking? Third, to whom or what are these obligations owed? Fourth, is the non-reciprocal nature of these obligations as much a feature of ecological citizenship as of its generic cousin, post-cosmopolitan citizenship? Informing the answer to each of these questions is the asymmetrical impact of different sized ecological footprints, and the corresponding obligation is to ensure that such footprints do not compromise or foreclose others' opportunities, both in the present and the future, for living meaningful lives. It is precisely the systematically asymmetrical nature of ecological footprint impact that gives rise to the non-reciprocity of the obligations they produce. All of this is indissolubly tied up with the matter of the virtues of ecological citizenship, and I turn to them now.

## Ecological Citizenship and Virtue

Citizenship theorists are fond of periodizing the development of citizenship, and most theorists are wedded to T. H. Marshall's periodization that, as I pointed out in Chapter 2, begins with civil citizenship and moves through political citizenship to social citizenship. The origins of Marshall's periodization are to

be found in the eighteenth century when the rights and freedoms necessary for the establishment of civil citizenship were
established: 'liberty of the person, freedom of speech, thought
and faith, the right to own property and to conclude valid
contracts, and the right to justice' (Rees 1996: 5). The influence
of Marshall's periodization has been so great that shifts in the
content of citizenship are usually shoehorned into his
timescale, even when the shoe does not fit, or when a broader
view would have given a better picture of what was going on.
Marshall's focus on rights does not allow us to 'see' the contemporary remoralization of politics and of citizenship because
rights are only very loosely connected with virtue. It is this,
I think, that prevented van Steenbergen from making as much
of ecological citizenship as he might have done (as I observed
earlier in the chapter), committed as he was to Marshall's
analytical and chronological framework.

As far as periodization is concerned, even Margaret Somers'
disputing Marshall's focus on 'capitalist revolutions and class
formation in the 17th and 18th centuries' in favour of
'medieval institutional and cultural foundations' (Somers
1994: 83) may not go back far enough, since Somers' attention
is still fixed on citizenship as rights-claiming. The contemporary
remoralization of politics and the significance of ecologism's
role in it only come properly into view if virtue-based citizenship is allowed into the timeframe, and this takes us back before
Marshall's eighteenth century, and even before Somers' Middle
Ages. In Chapter 2 we saw Peter Reisenberg distinguishing
between two sorts of citizenship, the first of which has its
roots in the very origins of citizenship as idea and practice:
'[T]he final centuries of the first citizenship had prepared the
way for the second... from the late Middle Ages on, lawyers
and political theorists had diminished the value of civic virtue
and stressed that of loyal and obedient subjectship' (Reisenberg
1992: 272). Virtue is the theme of the contemporary
remoralization of politics, and ecological citizenship, which in

Reisenberg's terms connects with the pre-Middle Age period, is a striking exemplar of it. The ecological citizen does the right thing not because of incentives, but because it is the right thing to do. In this sense the idea of ecological citizenship is one of the resources on which a society might draw to make itself more sustainable. As I pointed out in the introduction, Ludvig Beckman captures this very effectively. Let me repeat what he says:

the fact that the sustainability of the consumerist and individualist lifestyle is put into question undoubtedly raises a whole range of questions about how to reconstruct our society. What new economic and political institutions are needed? What regulations and set of incentives are necessary in order to redirect patterns of behaviour in sustainable directions... the question of sustainable behaviour cannot be reduced to a discussion about balancing carrots and sticks. The citizen that sorts her garbage or that prefers ecological goods will often do this because she feels committed to ecological values and ends. The citizen may not, that is, act in sustainable ways solely out of economic or practical incentives: people sometimes choose to do good for other reasons than fear (of punishment or loss) or desire (for economic rewards or social status). People sometimes do good because they want to be virtuous. (Beckman 2001: 179)

But just what does 'being virtuous' mean in this context? In Chapter 2, I triangulated the virtues of post-cosmopolitan citizenship by showing how it 'contained' the virtues of both liberal and civic republican citizenship, before arguing that in the post-cosmopolitan context it is not so much a question of which virtues are citizenship virtues, as of which kinds of relationships give rise to citizenship obligations. The virtues of post-cosmopolitan citizenship are, then, those virtues that enable these obligations to be met. The specific case of ecological citizenship tracks these more generic post-cosmopolitan points almost exactly. In the first place, then, we would expect ecological citizenship to 'contain' the virtues of liberal and civic republican citizenship, and indeed it does. Consider the following example from John Barry:

Citizenship, as viewed by green democratic theory, emphasizes the duty of citizens to take responsibility for their actions and choices—the obligation to 'do one's bit' in the collective enterprise of achieving sustainability. There is thus a notion of 'civic virtue' at the heart of this green conception of citizenship. A part of this notion of civic virtue refers to consideration of the interests of others and an openness to debate and deliberation. This implies that the duties of being a citizen go beyond the formal political realm, including, for example, such activities as recycling waste, ecologically aware consumption and energy conservation. (Barry 1999: 231)

Here Barry offers us explicit reference to both the liberal and civic republican traditions. The former is encapsulated in the reference to the virtue of 'an openness to debate and deliberation'. We will remember Will Kymlicka and Wayne Norman in Chapter 2 suggesting that 'public reasonableness' is a key liberal citizenship virtue: '[L]iberal citizens must give reasons for their political demands, not just state preferences or make threats' (Kymlicka and Norman 1994: 366), and Barry's idea is a very close replica of this. Civic republicanism is expressed through the idea of the 'collective enterprise' of achieving sustainability; this is a specific version of the 'common good' notion. Patrick Curry's 'ecological republicanism', to which I made reference earlier in the chapter, also resurrects the conception of virtue articulated by the civic republican tradition. 'It is fascinating to see the extent to which the perspective derived from civic republicanism is amenable to an ecological interpretation and expansion', he writes:

In so far as the common good of any human community is utterly dependent—not only ultimately but in many ways immediately—upon ecosystemic integrity (both biotic and abiotic), that integrity must surely assume pride of place in its definition. And it is only maintained by practices and duties of active 'citizenship', whose larger goal is the health not only of the human public sphere but of the natural world which encloses, sustains and constitutes it. Civic *virtù* is thus a subset of ecological *virtù*.                    (Curry 2000: 1067)

Curry deliberately relates the Machiavellian notion of *virtù* in its technical sense to the context of sustainability. As I pointed out earlier in the chapter, his argument is that, 'In the Machiavellian view, any community which values either aggressive private enterprise or passive personal salvation more than public service is well underway to disaster' (Curry 2000: 1062). And the sustainability point is that 'the ever-increasing damage inflicted upon the world's ecosystems for private profit, and which epitomises unsustainability, is a perfect instance of [Machiavellian] corruption' (Curry 2000: 1067). For Curry, in sum, sustainability is just the kind of common good that can be talked of in civic republican terms, and it requires the exercise of the kinds of virtues associated with that tradition.

These remarks serve to justify the claim that ecological citizenship contains the virtues typically associated with both liberal and civic republ-ican citizenship.

But it also goes beyond them—and it goes beyond them in the kind of way we saw in operation in the context of the generic analysis of post-cosmopolitan citizenship in Chapter 2. As we saw there, and as I remarked earlier in this section, it is not a matter of positing a series of virtues that are definitionally associated with such citizenship, but rather of attending to the conditions under which the obligations of citizenship are created, and via which, as a consequence, the virtues of such citizenship are called into play—whatever they may be. At this point the connections between this and two of the other dimensions of ecological citizenship we have discussed become apparent. It will be recalled that my point in the 'ecological non-territoriality' section was that the 'space' of ecological citizenship is created by the metabolistic relationship between individual human beings (and collections of them) and their non-human natural environment as they go about producing and reproducing their daily lives. This is the 'ecological footprint'.

Building on this in the section on 'duty and responsibility in ecological citizenship', I suggested that the ecological citizen's responsibility is 'to ensure that her or his ecological footprint does not compromise or foreclose the ability of others in present and future generations to pursue options important to them'.

It will be apparent from this that the first virtue of ecological citizenship is justice. More specifically, ecological citizenship virtue aims at ensuring a just distribution of ecological space. In contrast, John Barry has argued that 'It is relations of harm and vulnerability that underpin the community or network within which ecological stewardship and citizenship operate' (2002: 146). My view is that it is relations of systematic ecological injustice that give rise to the obligations of ecological citizenship. Vulnerability is a symptom of injustice rather than that which, in the first instance, generates networks of citizenship, and not all relations of vulnerability can be regarded as relations of citizenship. So my reference to a 'first' virtue of ecological citizenship is important and deliberate. With it, I intend to distinguish both between the foundational virtue of ecological citizenship and other virtues that may be instrumentally required by it, and also between virtue as Aristotelian 'dispositions of character' and *political* virtue. It is very common to see accounts of ecological virtue expressed in the Aristotelian idiom, but while this may be appropriate in broader contexts, I do not think it works in the specifically political context of citizenship. John Barry writes, for example, that:

Green politics, in basing itself upon a view of morality in which virtues are central, seeks to create what may be called 'symbiotic' rather than 'parasitic' social–environmental relations: that is, the cultivation of ecologically virtuous modes of interaction with the environment. The border between *symbiotic* and *parasitic* relations denotes the ethical border between use and abuse. Certain dispositions of character, and their social requirements, are held to be constitutive aspects of human–nature relations. Some of these virtues are peculiar to this domain of moral life, but some, perhaps the most important, such as sympathy or humanity, range over all aspects of morality.

(Barry 1999: 64)

I agree that 'virtues are central' to green politics—and to eco-logical citizenship—but I do not think that the 'dispositions of character' of which Barry speaks are the central virtues of eco-logical citizenship. The key virtue is, rather, justice—although I entirely agree that certain dispositions of character may be required to meet its demands. As I have pointed out on a num-ber of occasions here, we need to retain the distinction between the Good Samaritan and the Good Citizen, and the dispositions of character of which commentators on green politics often speak are usually more appropriately predicated of the former than they are of the latter. In the first instance at least, for example, Barry's 'sympathy' is a virtue appropriate to the Good Samaritan rather than to the Good Citizen.

Importantly, though, this leaves the possibility that sym-pathy, or other candidates such as care and compassion, might be regarded as ecological citizenship virtues *in the second instance*. This is to say that they might turn out to be important to the effective exercise of the first virtue, justice. Regarded in this way, as instruments in the service of ecological citizenship's principal virtue, Barry is absolutely right to point out that sec-ondary virtues can be drawn from a variety of unlikely sources:

citizenship is a practice within which ecologically beneficial varies such as self-reliance and self-restraint can be learnt and practised. Although green citizenship is politically based, the activities, values and principles it embodies are not confined to the political sphere as conventionally understood. The virtues one would expect to be embodied in this green form of responsible citizenship, as a form of moral character, would be operative in other spheres of human action and roles. (Barry 1999: 228)

The literature on citizenship and the environment is indeed peppered with references to virtues that one would not normally associate with citizenship, strictly construed. Hartley Dean, for example, writes that 'An ethic of care—whether it is defined as a feminist or an ecological ethic—provides the crucial link between an abstract principle of co-responsibility and the substantive practice by which we continually negotiate our rights and duties' (2001: 502), and Bart van Steenbergen, in the context of his critique of 'world' as opposed to 'earth' citizenship (see p. 98) argues that the 'notion of a global environmental manager is only a half-way house in the direction of what could be considered a real global ecological citizen, since what we are missing here is the notion of *care*' (1994*b*: 150, emphasis in the original).

We will remember from Chapter 2 that this is the kind of thing that renders Michael Ignatieff apoplectic: '[T]he pell-mell retreat from the language of justice to the language of caring is perhaps the most worrying sign of the decadence of the language of citizenship among all parties to the left of Mrs Thatcher' (Rees 1995: 321), and that 'the language of citizenship is not properly about compassion at all' (Ignatieff 1991: 34). It now becomes clear that the distinction Ignatieff draws between 'justice' and 'care' is inappropriate. This is not, in this instance, because I want to draw on the argument that justice is care, but because care (and compassion) will in some circumstances be the secondary virtues required for exercising ecological citizenship's first virtue, which is (distributive) justice. The proper exercise of compassion is a matter of casuistic judgement, since 'Compassion is always contextual ... its political applications require judgement in response to particularities, and as such they will properly escape the limitations of formal rules' (Whitebrook 2002: 542).

Care and compassion are, of course, typically associated with the private rather than the public sphere of human life. We saw John Barry, above, referring to 'the political sphere as conventionally understood', and to his view that 'The virtues one would expect to be embodied in this green form of responsible citizenship...would be operative in other spheres of human action and roles' (Barry 1999: 228). He goes on to say that 'The point about ecological stewardship is that the private sphere, when considered from an ecological point of view, moves from being a "non-political" to a political site of activity' (Barry 2002: 147–8). I agree, and I now take the opportunity to examine this point in more detail.

## The Private Realm in Ecological Citizenship

In Chapter 2 I concluded that the private realm is a crucial site of citizenship activity for post-cosmopolitan citizenship. This is so for two reasons. First, private acts can have public implications in ways that can be related to the category of citizenship. And second, some of the virtues of which we spoke in the previous section—care and compassion in particular, with their unconditional and non-reciprocal character—are characteristic of ideal–typical versions of private realm relationships.

In the specifically ecological context, it should be clear how private acts have public implications of a citizenship sort. We know that the conception of space around which ecological citizenship is organized is the ecological footprint. This footprint, in turn, is an expression of the impact that individuals and groups of individuals make on their environment. This impact is a function of the production and reproduction of individuals' lives, both of which have a private as well as a public dimension. The private sphere itself can be understood either as the physical space within which people's lives are produced and reproduced (such as apartments, houses, mobile homes), or the realm of relationships usually regarded as 'private' (such as those between friends and family). In a rough-and-ready sense, these dimensions of the private sphere correspond to the two ways in which the private realm can be related to ecological citizenship.

Consider, first, the private sphere as physical space. Earlier in the chapter I referred to Wackernagel's use of a city to illustrate how groups of humans living together draw on ecological space to sustain themselves. This is as true of the apartment, house, or mobile home as it is of the city. The house in which I am writing this book—or rather the people who live in it and make the decisions as to how to go about reproducing their lives—is a maker of ecological footprints, and therefore a potential source of the generation of the kinds of responsibilities that I argued in the first section of this chapter can be associated with ecological citizenship. (I say 'potential' because obviously not all private spaces are in ecological space debt.) This is of course true of the 'public' spaces in which people work as well as the private spaces in which they live. The university where I work, for example, is also an occupier of ecological space, and taking my responsibilities as an ecological citizen seriously would involve me working to reduce the ecological space it occupies. But this just goes to show how odd it would be to regard my eco-political activities in the university as acts of citizenship and deny the description to similar acts at home, driven as they are by the same source of obligation. Let me try to drive this point home by referring once again to a point made in Chapter 2, where we saw Ruth Lister endorsing the traditional public/private distinction drawn by Anne Phillips, in which 'campaigning in public for men to do their fair share of the housework' is regarded as citizenship and 'simply sorting out the division of labour in one's home' is not (Lister 1997: 28). Whatever the case in the context of feminism, from an ecological point of view such a distinction leads to counter-intuitive conclusions. It would mean, for example, that campaigning for recycling centres is citizenship, but composting in one's own garden is not. This cannot be right: the point is that all green actions in the home have a public impact, in the specific sense of the creation of an ecological footprint. This, in turn, potentially generates the kinds of obligations I have said we should associate with ecological citizenship.

The second way of understanding 'the private' is in terms of the realm of relationships normally designated as such. This includes friendship and relationships within families. Now, such relationships can of course be extremely damaging and dysfunctional, but the important thing from my point of view is that we regard 'damage' and 'dysfunction' in quite specific ways in these contexts. Baldly, such relationships are ideally regarded as involving unconditionality and non-reciprocity. We do not love our children because we want something in return from them, any more than we stop buying gifts for friends because they do not buy us one in return. The connection between this and ecological citizenship should be clear. I argued earlier in the chapter that a characteristic feature of the obligations of ecological citizenship is their non-reciprocity. Since this is also a definitional feature of relationships normally associated with the private sphere, the relationship between ecological citizenship and the private sphere is a tight one. This is more than just a question of analogy, since it extends into the very territory of virtue. We saw in the previous section that certain virtues not normally associated with citizenship turn out to be important to the exercise of ecological citizenship, in the second order sense of being necessary to instantiate its first order virtue—that of justice. Two of the virtues mentioned there were care and compassion—virtues typically related to the private realm. Perhaps this is the kind of thing Peter Christoff refers to as a 'green conscience': 'For its success, the emancipatory project which is shaped by—and in turn constitutes—ecological citizens depends on the revitalisation and extension of civil society. It depends upon the active transformation of private life through creation of a "green conscience" . . . '(Christoff 1996: 162). In my own terms, the 'green conscience' has its very material origins in the differential impacts of ecological footprints, but is certainly cashed out—in part at least—in terms of the 'private' virtues sometimes required to do 'public' justice.

In sum, then, the private realm is important to ecological citizenship because it is a site of citizenship activity, and because the kinds of obligations it generates, and the virtues necessary to meeting those obligations, are analogously and actually present in the types of relationship we normally designate as 'private'. Although this is counter-intuitive in respect of the vast bulk of work done on citizenship in general, it is absolutely consistent with what political ecologists take citizenship to be about. Ecological citizenship is an encumbered citizenship, far removed, on one level at least, from gendered civic republicanism and its contemporary manifestations: 'the ideal citizen of classical republicanism . . . was largely freed from the necessity to labour and to meet his bodily requirements . . . unencumbered by the demands of everyday living' (Lister 1997: 32). Ecological citizenship, in contrast, is *all about* everyday living. In Chapter 2 I pointed out how the private realm is systematically subordinated to the public realm by associating citizenship exclusively with the latter at the same time as according it (citizenship) a privileged status. In this context, I noted, the acquisition of citizenship is read as an escape from the realm of 'necessity' (the private realm) into the realm of 'freedom' (public citizenship). We saw Gershon Shafir write that:

In the context of the Greek city-state, the *polis*, citizenship appeared as a double process of emancipation . . . it was the transcendence of the instrumental sphere of necessity, in which we toil to satisfy our material wants, into the sphere of freedom . . . This contrast has been conceptualised in multiple forms—for example, as emancipation from the private sphere of the household (*oikos*) into the public sphere of political life (*polis*). (Shafir 1998: 3)

It should be clear from our discussion here how ecological citizenship resists this interpretation of 'emancipation'. The 'sphere of necessity' cannot be transcended, since it is the sphere where much of the production and reproduction of human life takes place. The 'sphere of freedom' implicit in

Shafir's gloss is an impossibilist sphere in which we live on thin air. In the terms I have deployed in this chapter, 'toiling to satisfy our material wants' amounts to the production of ecological footprints which, far from removing us from the realm of citizenship, actually generates the kinds of obligations peculiar to it.

## Conclusion

In this chapter I hope to have shown how the post-cosmopolitan citizenship sketched in the first chapter takes a specifically modulated form in the ecological context. Ecological citizenship is therefore both an example of post-cosmopolitan citizenship and a particular interpretation of it. It possesses all the basic features of post-cosmopolitan citizenship, such as its stress on responsibilities rather than rights, and its determination to regard these responsibilities as non-reciprocal rather then contractual, thus contrasting with both liberal and civic republican understandings of citizenship obligations. It also focuses on virtue as being central to citizenship, but once again differs markedly from both liberal and civic republican articulations in its sense that these virtues need to be drawn from the private as well as the public arenas. Similarly, it unusually regards the private arena as a legitimate site of citizenship activity, both because the kinds of relationship normally associated with that arena are similar in content to those of ecological citizenship, and because the private realm generates the space—the ecological footprint—that gives rise to the obligations of ecological citizenship itself.

For liberals, this politicization of the private sphere will sound an alarm. Mark Smith is surely right to point out that 'Many basic personal choices which were previously considered inviolable will be subject to challenge' (1998: 99). This, in turn, is a challenge to liberalism. If the sustainable society is a worthwhile social objective—and most states, liberal or otherwise, subscribe to it at least in name—then liberal polities must find a way of engaging the resources of citizenship in order to achieve it. This, though, seems to bring two issues to the fore with which liberal polities traditionally have great difficulty: the politicization of the private sphere and the idea of the 'good life'. Does the pursuit of a sustainable society necessarily involve the endorsement of a determinate view of the right way to live? And, if so, how can liberal states pursue it, given the ground rule of neutrality as far as the good life is concerned? More particularly, how can education systems in liberal states teach ecological citizenship if so many of its tenets seem opposed to liberal principles? These are the questions that animate the rest of this book.

# Chapter 4

# Environmental Sustainability in Liberal Societies

I have outlined the intellectual and political need for a new type of citizenship and sketched what this 'post-cosmopolitanism' might look like (Chapters 1 and 2). In Chapter 3 I offered ecological citizenship as a specific articulation of this new citizenship. My intention in the present chapter is to reflect on the place of ecological citizenship in liberal societies as a prelude to (in Chapter 5) examining a particular way of instantiating it in such societies, through the formal education system. Two preliminary questions present themselves: why the focus on liberal societies?, and why the slippage indicated in the title of this chapter from 'ecological citizenship' to 'environmental sustainability'?

The first question is prompted by the thought that most countries in the world do not have liberal democratic characteristics, and many of these have no pretensions to them either.

What, then, can be the general relevance of such a narrow focus? One answer to the question is that whatever their general relevance, liberal societies (broadly speaking) are those that I know best and can therefore comment upon most knowledgeably. This has always been a legitimate defence of selecting one type of political system or regime for case-study analysis in comparative politics. Another answer—closer to the heart of the matter—is that the instantiation of environmental sustainability raises especially interesting questions in the context of liberal societies. This is because some argue that practising sustainability inevitably involves living some determinate version of 'the good life', yet one of the defining claims of the liberal state is that it is neutral between competing views of what living the good life entails. How can the liberal state deliver sustainability, in other words, if it has to do so with one arm tied behind its back? This question provides the thread that runs through this chapter and Chapter 5. A final answer to the question of why focus on liberal democratic societies is probably the most important one, and it is linked to the second, but is not the one on which I shall focus here. The answer, simply, is that while liberal democracies may be in the minority as far as political systems across the world are concerned, they are responsible for by far the most environmental damage (although this does not of course necessarily make liberal democracy the proximate cause of such damage). This is especially true of global environmental problems, such as global warming, ozone layer depletion, and the decline of major oceanic fish stocks. It is particularly important, therefore, that environmental sustainability feature in the warp and weft of liberal democratic societies—and this brings us straight back to the second issue raised a moment ago: how can 'the good' be instantiated in societies that are ideologically committed to correct procedures rather than substantive outcomes?

The second question was: why the slippage from 'ecological citizenship' to 'environmental sustainability'? Part of the answer

is that even if there is a slippage, I shall return to ecological citizenship in Chapter 5 where I examine it in the context of citizenship education. The other part of the answer is that I do not
consider it a slippage anyway. In Chapter 3, while discussing
the distinction between environmental and ecological citizenship, I said that 'I regard environmental and ecological citizenship
as complementary in that while they organise themselves on
different terrains, they can both plausibly be read as heading
in the same direction: the sustainable society' (p. 68). Ecological
citizenship and environmental sustainability are therefore
bound together in a rather obvious way, in that the former is a
potential means for achieving the latter. I hope that these
preliminaries are sufficient to convince the reader that instantiating environmental sustainability in liberal societies is a topic
worth thinking about, and that doing so is central to the book's
topic of citizenship and the environment.

The question that animates this chapter and Chapter 5, then,
is whether environmental sustainability can legitimately be
instantiated in liberal societies, with special reference to the
formal education system in such societies. As I suggested above,
some will argue that it cannot. The argument runs as follows:

(a) environmental sustainability is about norms as well as
    techniques;
(b) liberal states must be neutral in respect of norms for
    living; therefore,
(c) the formal machinery of the liberal state (e.g. the education
    system) should not favour one norm for living over
    others; so,
(d) education for ecological citizenship cannot effectively be
    delivered by the state in liberal societies.

There are a number of ways of interrupting the flow of this
argument and most of them will focus on parts (a) and (b). It
might be argued in the context of (a), for example, that environmental sustainability is not about norms at all, but is a matter for

scientific determination, no more and no less. On this reading, thresholds of sustainability are a matter for scientific ecologists, not for social scientists—and much less for philosophers and the public at large. I think this argument is wrong, and I shall spend some time in what follows explaining why.

As for (b), all sorts of sophisticated things have been said about claims regarding liberal neutrality, most of them intended to undermine the claim itself. This debate formed the backdrop to an important exchange of views between Piers Stephens and Marcel Wissenburg (Stephens 2001a,b; Wissenburg 2001) on the relationship between liberalism and the environment, organized around a discussion of Wissenburg's path-breaking book on the subject (Wissenburg 1998). Stephens says that part of the problem with Wissenburg's 'argument for the capacity of the liberal democratic state to deliver much of the green agenda' (Stephens 2001a: 1) is that he (Wissenburg) accepts too readily 'the definition of a liberal state as being one which is neutral between competing conceptions of the good' (Stephens 2001a: 3). There are at least two problems with this, says Stephens, rehearsing arguments made elsewhere and by others in response to liberalism's neutrality claim. The first is that liberalism does not live up to its own standards. So Stephens argues that:

There must . . . be reasons, either directly or indirectly to do with some formulation of citizens' welfare, as to why neutrality is the correct procedure, and . . . I . . . argue that such a formulation will itself be value-laden and necessarily involve either overt or covert recourse to regulative ideals of human nature, to what a human being is and what they may or ideally ought to become.                (Stephens 2001a: 4)

The second kind of response is that even if we grant the aspiration of neutrality to some kinds of liberalism, and even if we accept that this aspiration is a practical one, we should not accept that liberalism as a political ideology is wholly and completely describable in terms of such neutrality. This is to say there are other kinds of liberalism too. As Stephens points out: 'Though the notion of neutrality does indeed appear to articulate long-standing liberal concerns. It is well worth recognising that the use of this rather abstract team as a defining characteristic of liberalism is...a recent development...[Jeremy] Waldron sees no explicit formulation in these terms before 1974' (Stephens 2001a: 5). Reference is often made in this context to so-called 'perfectionist' liberalism, and contrasts are also drawn between the liberalism of John Locke (bad) and John Stuart Mill (good), for example (Stephens 2001a: 6–10). In terms of interrupting the flow of the argument (a)–(d) outlined above, this 'excavation' of the liberal heritage is a useful gambit. For if it can be shown that liberalism is not definitionally wedded to neutrality then there may be room for liberal states to articulate, legitimately, determinate views of the good life. Even if we accept proposition (a), then, that environmental sustainability involves normative as well as scientific judgements, a re-reading of liberalism might yet allow a liberal education system to deliver a determinate normative framework for living—see point (d), above.

The normal place, then, to install a red traffic light (or at least an amber one) on the road that carries us inexorably to the conclusion that education for ecological citizenship cannot be effectively delivered by the state in liberal societies is at point (b) in the argument, where neutrality in respect of norms is regarded as a key feature of the liberal state. In this chapter I want to try a different and much less explored strategy. In brief, and contrary to the received wisdom of those who wish to make liberalism and environmental sustainability compatible, I propose that we *accept* point (b) exactly as 'neutralist' liberals would wish, that is, that the liberal state should be neutral in respect of norms for living. I do not think, though, that this commits us to accepting the conclusion at (d)—that education for ecological citizenship cannot effectively be delivered in liberal societies. In arguing against this conclusion I hope not only to provide a novel 'take' on the liberalism–sustainability relationship, but also to show how liberalism's commitment to neutrality creates obligations to its citizens—particularly in the realm of citizenship education—which it generally comes nowhere near to fulfilling. Allow me, though, to keep the rabbit in the hat a while longer, and to get the argument going with a defence of point (a) in the argument outlined earlier, that is, that environmental sustainability is about norms as well as techniques.

## The Normative Nature of Environmental Sustainability

I confess surprise that there is still a debate as to whether environmental sustainability is a matter of norms or of scientific determination. Most readers of this book will likely agree with me that sustainability is a normative notion and will therefore wonder at my devoting a section of this chapter to arguing that it is. Has not this been conclusively established? Well, my experiences talking formally and informally to the policy community suggest that no, it has not—or at least not in the systematic and internalized way that would make a difference to policy formulation (or, pertinently, to how it is taught in secondary and high schools—see Chapter 5). I admit that my policy community conversations are mostly confined to the United Kingdom, but I see no obvious reason why they should differ substantially from those that might take place elsewhere. The litmus test, I have found, is how people react to the term 'threshold'. This is a key term in sustainability debates, where a threshold refers to the borderline between a sustainable and an unsustainable state of affairs. Time and again I am told in these fora that thresholds are most appropriately determined by natural scientists because they possess the investigative tools and knowledges required to determine them most accurately. One small question, though, is sufficient to unsettle this cosy consensus: a threshold for whom or for what? Scientists will only be able to tell us that practice P is likely to push us over a threshold once we have told him/her to whom or to what the threshold applies (human beings or parakeets?), and this cannot be determined by science alone. Different degrees of human intervention in an ecosystem will have different impacts on the biotic and abiotic elements in that system. It might be thought that the question of which of these elements 'matter', and therefore which of them should be preserved or otherwise sustained, can only be answered by scientific investigation. But deciding which elements 'matter' is itself a normative as well as a scientific affair.

As far as 'defining' sustainability is concerned, Brian Barry is surely right to say that 'The core concept of sustainability is... that there is some X whose value should be maintained, in as far as it lies within our power to do so, into the indefinite future'. He goes on to point out that 'This leaves it open for dispute what the content of X should be' (B. Barry 1999: 101). It should be clear by now that this dispute is not only over what X might be, but also how to determine what kind of thing it is—determinable by scientific investigation, or through normative debate? Likewise, Barry asks us to:

suppose that concern about sustainability takes its origins from the suspicion...That we are shortchanging our successors. If we then take this to mean that we should not act in such a way as to leave them with less of what matters than we enjoy, and call that sustainability, it is clear that the content of sustainability will depend crucially on what we think matters. (B. Barry 1999: 101)

Once again, 'what matters' cannot be determined by science alone.

Barry offers an instructive example of the way in which, as far as sustainability is concerned, what appear to be matters of fact are actually matters of interpretation. 'Consider especially the arguments in the literature about the status of "natural capital" ', he says (B. Barry 1999: 102). 'Natural capital' is one common answer to the question of what should be sustained into the future, but there are those who argue that this is unnecessary since all the functions performed by natural capital can be performed by substitutes. This is a belief in 'fungibility'. Barry goes on:

> For someone who adopts want-satisfaction as a criterion, all resources are in principle fungible: if plastic trees are as satisfying as real ones, there is no reason for worrying about the destruction of the world's trees so long as the resources exist to enable plastic replacements to be manufactured in sufficient numbers. Those who insist that 'natural capital' must be preserved are in effect denying the complete fungibility of all capital. But what is this disagreement actually about? On the interpretation I wish to offer, this is not a disagreement that turns on some matter of fact. It would be quite possible to agree with everything that might be said in favour of fungibility and still deny that it amounts to a case against the special status of 'natural capital'. For the case in favour of giving the preservation of nature an independent value is that it is important in its own right. If future people are to have access to what matters, and unspoilt nature is an essential part of what matters, then it follows that loss of 'natural capital' cannot be traded off against any amount of additional productive capacity.
>
> (B. Barry 1999: 102–3)

Barry's point is that arguments against fungibility and in favour of the preservation of natural capital are usually couched in terms of the impossibility of fungibility; the idea, that is, that natural capital is simply *not* permanently and systematically replaceable by man-made substitutes. While this may be true, says Barry, it misses the normative point. The key thing, he argues, is that even if we accept the possibility of fungibility we might not accept its desirability. The content of sustainability's X, in other words, cannot be determined by the 'facts' alone.

It would be wrong to think that the policy-making community is driven by a naive commitment to fact- and science-based solutions to defining sustainability, however. In Britain, at least, the various government departments, commissions, and committees most closely connected with these debates are showing welcome signs of grappling with the difficulties that recognition of the normative nature of sustainability brings in its train. The best that can be said, though, is that messages in this context are still mixed: the normative nature of sustainability is regarded as an annoying feature that just has to be dealt with, rather than its central and defining characteristic. Let me offer one or two examples to substantiate this claim, and then comment upon its importance for the general issue of instantiating environmental sustainability in liberal societies.

The Aarhus Convention on Access to Information, Public Participation in Decision-Making and Access to Justice in Environmental Matters (1998) is widely regarded as one of the most important agreements ever reached by European governments in the environmental context. The details of the agreement do not matter here, but it is worth pointing out the normative assumptions contained in its general remit. In its preamble, the Convention refers approvingly to the 'Stockholm Declaration on the Human environment', and to the United Nations General Assembly's resolution 45/94 on 'the need to ensure a healthy environment for the well-being of individuals' (Aarhus Convention 1998: 1). In combination, these two statements effectively take a stance on what we earlier established was a key normative moment in the definition of sustainability—determining for whom, or for what, sustainability thresholds are to be implemented. The individuals whose well-being is to be ensured are evidently human individuals. I make no judgement of this stance here; I merely point it out as an example of the normative underpinnings of environmental agreements to which governments often sign up in our name. And this makes a real difference in terms of policy implementation, since environmental impact assessments carried out in advance of building work, for example, will come to very different conclusions depending on whom or what the impact might affect.

Laudably, the Aarhus Convention goes on to affirm the need to 'protect, preserve and improve the state of the environment' (Aarhus Convention 1998: 1). It does not take a moral philosopher, though, to see that the idea of 'improvement' takes us into a normative minefield. How do we know when an improvement in the environment has taken place? More generally, how do we know when we have more sustainability rather than less of it? Most pertinently: are we prepared to accept that there is no determinate answer to these questions? Something of the British government's view of these matters can be gleaned from its list of sustainable development objectives and indicators. One of its objectives is 'maintaining high and stable levels of economic growth and employment', and one of its indicators in this regard is 'GDP and GDP per head' (UK Government 2002). Another of its objectives is 'effective protection of the environment', and one measure of this is 'rivers of good or fair quality' (UK Government 2002). Now these two objectives, both of which are intended to be compatible parts of a general framework, might uncharitably be regarded as competing rather than compatible versions of what 'improvement' means. This becomes especially apparent when we see that Gross Domestic Product (GDP) is an extremely blunt instrument for determining the health of an economy. GDP, as environmentalists never tire of pointing out (e.g. see Anderson 1991), is a measure of *every* activity carried out in an economy—including clearing up environmental damage once it has occurred. There is the possibility, then, that an event which pulls down one sustainable development indicator— a discharge of effluent into a river, for example—will register as a bonus on another (the increased economic activity associated with cleaning up the mess). At the very least, then, there are mixed messages as far as the British government's view of 'improvement' in the context of sustainable development is concerned. Following Brian Barry, above, this tension cannot be characterized as a dispute over facts. It is perfectly possible to think that there might be no disagreement over the measurement of economic growth and of river quality, and for there still to be a debate about their relative merits as indicators of sustainability.

There can be little doubt, though, that things are moving in the right direction as far as the British government, at least, is concerned. The Royal Society (independent of government, of course) points out in its report on genetically modified plants for food use and human health, for example, that 'Some respondents raised social and ethical concerns about GM technology' (Royal Society 1998: 4), but then tries to separate out these concerns from the 'pure science' by saying that 'We have confined ourselves to commenting on the scientific issues involved in genetic modification of plants because this is where our expertise lies' (Royal Society 1998: 4). Officially, at least, the British government is sceptical of this kind of distinction. In its response to the Royal Commission's landmark Report on Environmental Pollution, the Department of the Environment, Food and Rural Affairs (DEFRA) points out that 'it is ... important for science to understand how its own values affect what it does' (DEFRA 2000: II, 22). It might have referred for evidence for this view to the Royal Society's take on the notorious idea of 'substantial equivalence', according to which 'if a novel or GM food can be shown to be essentially equivalent in composition to an existing food then it can be considered as safe as its conventional equivalent' (Royal Society 1998: 5). The Royal Society judges equivalence in terms of toxicology and nutrition, but there is obviously a host of other factors to be taken into account. One does not have to be an anthropologist of food to see that cultural issues are also key to determining 'equivalence'—and the Royal Society seems to acknowledge as much when it rather lamely concludes that: 'The amount of comparative data required to establish comparative equivalence involves a somewhat subjective judgement' (Royal Society 1998: 5–6).

Perhaps the best way to substantiate my claim that an awareness of the normative nature of sustainability in policy-making circles has yet to be converted into a principled and integrated feature of the decision-making process, is to show how values come into the process too late. Governments around the world grapple with the problem of 'environmental standards', and with just how to determine what these standards should be. There is an understandable desire to base standards on 'objective criteria', and the British government constantly refers to 'evidence-based policy making' as a shorthand for such criteria (DEFRA 2000: I, 5). But the real question, of course, is what are to count as criteria in the first place. Of course scientific testimony will count, but bearing in mind everything we have said about the irreducibly normative nature of sustainability, should not values be captured and offered as evidence too?

Sometimes government seems to be aware of the need to allow values to count as evidence. I referred earlier to the UK government's list of sustainable development objectives (there are four: 'social progress which recognises the needs of everyone', 'effective protection of the environment', 'prudent use of natural resources', 'maintenance of high and stable levels of economic growth and employment'; UK Government 2002). I pointed out that there are likely to be tensions between these objectives, and it is important to see that these tensions cannot be resolved solely through the application of science. The British government seems to recognize as much:

The Government believes that the need for integrated thinking, which is at the heart of sustainable development, will lead to better environmental standard-setting. As the Royal Commission [in its Report on Environmental Pollution] points out, 'there is much debate about the relative weight that should be placed on the different elements within the overall balance sustainable development is intended to achieve.'

Such debate will continue. But thinking in terms of sustainable development can help to define priorities, build consensus and identify opportunities for multiple benefits.                    (DEFRA 2000: II, 15)

The idea of 'relative weight' acknowledges the tensions between the four objectives, and the reference to 'debate' suggests something other than decision by scientific fiat.

The apparent official determination to regard values as evidence is even clearer in the following:

In launching its report, the Royal Commission said that a new approach was needed such that 'as well as drawing on rigorous and dispassionate analysis, there must be a greater sensitivity to people's values. It must recognise that scientific assessments, and analyses of technology, economics and risk, must inform policy decisions, but cannot pre-empt them. Setting a standard or target is not only a scientific or technical matter, but also a practical judgement which has to be made in the light of all the relevant factors. People's values must be taken into account from the earliest stages of defining the problem and framing the questions that need to be addressed'. The Government fully endorses this conclusion.                    (DEFRA 2000: II, 21)

Reading passages like this, one could be forgiven for thinking that government and its advisers had fully grasped the normative dimension of sustainability and was determined to factor it into decision-making as far as the setting of environmental standards is concerned. And just in case some cynics remain unconvinced, DEFRA underscores the importance of taking values into account when setting agendas and when framing the very questions to be asked:

Values have to play a part not only in the synthesis, but also—as the Commission recognise—in deciding what constitutes a 'problem', and in framing the questions for analysis. The Government agrees that better ways need to be found to articulate people's values. As part of the Modernising Government agenda it has established a People's Panel to give one indication of the way individuals perceive certain issues. As part of the reform of the regulatory system for genetically modified organisms the Government is setting up an Agriculture and Environment Biotechnology Commission which will consider not only scientific but also ethical and social questions raised by genetically-modified organisms.

(DEFRA 2000: III, 27)

It would be churlish to try to argue that all this is not a massive improvement on the belief that the nature of sustainability can be determined in scientific laboratories. But there are signs that the transformation is not quite complete. One sign is the reference to the 'articulation' of people's values in the last quotation. Environmentalists have long argued that forums for discussing these matters should allow for the development of people's values as well as their articulation. There may be more values present in the case, in other words, than those articulated in any given forum. Other signs come more explicitly from the selfsame document from which I have been quoting. Commenting on the need to determine which bits of the environment are most in need of protection, for example, DEFRA writes that:

Environmental standard setting cannot aim to protect every bit of the environment for ever. But the Government aims to prevent further overall deterioration, and to secure enhancements that contribute to an overall improvement in quality of life. Environmental capital techniques, which help us understand which aspects of the environment are important, and why, can be useful aids to some types of environmental decision making.

(DEFRA 2000: II, 18)

The reference to 'environmental capital techniques' here is a nod in the direction of the idea of 'natural capital', according to which (as mentioned earlier) some of the 'services' provided by nature cannot be adequately delivered by human-made substitutes. These, in other words, are the 'aspects of the environment [that] are important' for policy-making purposes.

It is not the difficulty of determining just where the line ought to be drawn on which I want to comment here, but the idea of referring to the environment in terms of 'capital' at all.

In earlier quotations from this key DEFRA document we have seen a laudable determination to 'get values in' as early as possible—at the point of the very framing of the question indeed. Referring to the environment in terms of 'capital', though, violates this rule of thumb. Brian Barry is surely right to say that:

> 'Capital' is a term that is inherently located within economic discourse. A mountain is, in the first instance, just a mountain. To bring it under the category of 'capital'—of any kind—is to look it in a certain light, as an economic asset of some description. But if I want to insist that we should leave future generations mountains that have not been strip-mined, quarried, despoiled by ski-slopes, or otherwise tampered with to make somebody a profit, my point will be better made by eschewing talk about 'capital' altogether.     (B. Barry 1999: 103).

There is of course no such thing as an entirely value-free language in which to discuss the X of sustainability (or anything else for that matter), but 'capital' is surely one of the more obviously loaded categories available to us. While a tomato may be regarded as capital in that it can be bought and sold, its value can be expressed in other ways too (it has a nice smell, you can write poems about it, and so on). A thoroughgoing application of the rule to get values in at the earliest opportunity would have led to some commentary, at least, on the implications of using 'capital' to describe the environment.

Let me offer one more example of where the official guard is let down. Remember the injunction that 'People's values must be taken into account from the earliest stages of defining the problem and framing the questions that need to be addressed' (DEFRA 2000: II, 21), then consider the following key stages in risk assessment from the British government's 'Guidelines for Environmental Risk Assessment and Management' (apologies for quoting them in full, but this is the best way of making the point). Look, in particular, for the first explicit reference to 'value judgements':

- **hazard identification:** identifying the potential for harm. This will have an important bearing on the overall assessment. It is important not to overlook secondary hazards that may arise—for example, during flooding contaminated sediments might be deposited on agricultural land;

- **identification of consequences:** identifying the potential consequences that may arise from any given hazard—at this stage no account is taken of likely exposure and therefore likely consequences;
- **estimation of the magnitude of consequences:** these can be actual or potential harm to human health, property or the natural environment. Estimation needs to take into account geographical scale and duration of consequences, and how quickly harmful effects might be seen. Long-term problems must be considered as well as immediate risks;
- **estimating the probability of consequences:** taking into account the probability of a hazard occurring, and of harm resulting;
- **evaluating the significance of a risk:** having determined the probability and magnitude of the consequences, it is important to place them in context. At this point some value judgements are made, either through reference to some pre-existing measure, such as a toxicological threshold or environmental quality standards, or reference to social, ethical or political standards. In some circumstances, a formalised quantitative approach to determining significance may be possible, for example the tolerability of risk frameworks developed by the Health and Safety Executive. In other instances, the risks of various options might be compared against one another;
- **options appraisal:** considering whether to reject, accept or reduce the risk, or to mitigate the effects.

(DEFRA 2000: VI, 69)

The first explicit reference to values occurs in the fifth of six stages of risk assessment, which hardly amounts to taking people's values into account 'from the earliest stages of defining the problem and framing the questions that need to be addressed'. I offer this as evidence for my view that 'while there is an awareness of the normative nature of sustainability in policy-making circles, this has yet to be converted into a principled and integrated feature of the decision-making process' (p. 152).

As Marcel Wissenburg has wisely pointed out, 'Facts, no matter how many facts, are meaningless without means of interpreting them—without a moral point of view' (Wissenburg 1998: 224). The evidence I have presented here suggests a government struggling with the implications of this in the tricky territory of environmental sustainability. This happens to be evidence drawn from the British government, but there is no reason to suggest that things will be much different elsewhere. If I say that there is a struggle at the heart of government over the place of values in the sustainability conundrum, this is no longer to say (thank goodness) that there is an argument over *whether* values are relevant or not, but rather over how to come to terms with the dawning recognition that they are relevant. This is tremendously important; not only in terms of sustainability itself, but also in terms of how the government fulfils its obligations to its citizens. As I pointed out earlier, the British government is a signatory to the Aarhus Convention, and has thereby committed itself to publishing the 'facts and analyses of facts which it considers relevant and important in framing major environmental policy proposals' (Aarhus Convention 1998: 9). At one level the government is clearly fulfilling this obligation (e.g. see UK Government 2002). But just how is the injunction to present 'analyses of facts' to be most fully interpreted? If we take the normative nature of sustainability seriously, these analyses must surely contain explicit and systematic reference to the values present in 'facts'. Such analyses would point out the anthropocentric nature of the Aarhus Convention, for example, and would recognize that 'environmental capital techniques' for determining which bits of the environment to protect are themselves in need of a little normative 'analysis'.

The 'analyses of facts' to which the government has committed itself, then, should be richly textured and must refer to the normative questions raised by the objective of sustainable development. There are signs that the government is not wholly ill-equipped to offer such analyses, but there is definitely room for improvement. How to improve? One way might be to offer the following key sustainability formulation from Marcel Wissenburg (his 'restraint principle') to policy-makers and ask them to discuss what 'unless unavoidable' means: 'no goods shall be destroyed unless unavoidable and unless they are replaced by perfectly identical goods; if that is physically impossible, they should be replaced by equivalent goods resembling the original as closely as possible; and if that is also impossible, a proper compensation should be provided' (Wissenburg 1998: 123).

Another way to create a greater demand and supply of richer 'analyses of facts' in the environmental context is through using the formal education system to produce citizens who both want such analyses and are capable of negotiating the normative demands they involve. But can the liberal state produce such citizens without violating its commitment to value neutrality? If it is true that 'a greener liberalism will have to define more clearly what kind of sustainability, what kind of world, it aims for' (Wissenburg 1998: 81), then will this not commit it irrevocably to a determinate view of the good life, and will it not, at this point, no longer be a liberal state? We are now in a position to devote the rest of this chapter, and much of Chapter 5 to answering this question.

## The Liberal State and Normative Neutrality

In the search for compatibility between liberalism and ecologism, the avowed aim of the liberal state's neutrality as regards norms for the good life has been a major stumbling block. Derek Bell sums up the situation as follows:

both sides [i.e. those who argue that liberalism is compatible with environmentalism and those who argue that it is not] tend to agree on one issue, namely, if liberalism is understood to include the idea of neutrality, liberalism is incompatible with environmentalism. The claim is that in promoting an environmentalist agenda the state would be promoting a particular conception of the good life but liberal neutrality requires that the state should not support any particular conception of 'the good life'. (Bell 2002: 704)

Bell also provides us with a useful checklist of the types of neutrality we might want to talk about:

1. Neutrality of effect: institutional arrangements and state policies should be designed so that all comprehensive ideals are similarly affected.
2. Substantive state neutrality: the state must not offer (or accept) comprehensive arguments as justifications for policy.
3. Fundamental neutrality: a political conception of justice (including a decision-making procedure) must not be justified by appealing to arguments or assumptions drawn from comprehensive doctrines. (Bell 2002: 718)

It is the second of these that most interests me here and in Chapter 5, since it bears more closely than the other two on the use of the state's formal education system to pursue a specific normative agenda—in this case, the agenda related to achieving environmental sustainability.

I pointed out near the beginning of the chapter that there are two main ways of trying to bypass the neutrality objection to compatibility between liberalism and ecologism. Let me remind us of these arguments before proceeding to an alternative strategy—one which simultaneously renders liberalism more compatible with ecologism than we might expect, but at the cost of demanding far more from the liberal state (up to an including the formal education system) than it is currently in the habit of providing.

The first 'bypass' strategy, it will be remembered, was to deny that neutrality as regards norms for living is as fundamental to the liberal prospectus as is often claimed. If this is true, then evidently the way is open to draw on traditions in liberalism that allow—even perhaps enjoin—the liberal state to pursue defin-itive versions of the good life. This might be called the 'anyone-but-Locke' move, and Piers Stephen offers a typical version of it when he writes that 'Mill's [John Stuart, that is] work...is surely the classical liberal theory with which greens can find common ground' (Stephens 2001*a*: 10).

The second strategy is to deny that any version of liberalism is neutral as regards the good life anyway. On this reading, any corner of the carpet you turn up will reveal a version of the good life lurking underneath. Thus Stephens, again, writes that 'liberalism may be agnostic as to the nature of the good life, but it must contain some conception of the necessary requirements for a good life; as Rawls would put it, it must have a notion of primary goods' (Stephens 2001*a*: 4). More specifi-cally, 'Locke, for all his status as an icon of liberal toleration, had no time for the conceptions of freedom held by the folk tradi-tions of sylvan liberty, and was a fervent apologist for enclosure and Baconian agricultural improvements that would maximise production' (Stephens 2001*a*: 6). This, argues Stephens, involves Locke in articulating a view of the good life *malgré lui*:

Locke, then, had little doubt about the existence of an objective good, and was strongly convinced of the character of this good. In relation to the goal of state neutrality noted earlier, we can see...that the state may be granted additional powers to promote a core goal, that of a par-ticular conception of liberty, a conception which closely ties liberty and moral rationality to a dynamic of transformative labour. Locke's praise of the industrious farmer who maximises production could not be more explicit on this transformative dynamic; it is, he informs us, '*Labour* indeed that *puts the difference of value* on everything', use-value being 99 per cent 'on the account of labour', whereas 'Land that is wholly left to Nature' is 'called, as indeed it is, wast'.

(Stephens 2001*a*: 6–7)

If we cast our minds back to Brian Barry's view that 'the content of sustainability will depend crucially on what we think mat-ters' (B. Barry 1999: 101), we can see that Locke is indeed here taking a stance on 'what matters'. If we were to ask him what he would want to pass on to future generations, 'wast' would come somewhere near the bottom of his list. For him, land mixed with labour is more valuable than land 'left to Nature'. Stephens concludes that 'the system, though not attempting to enforce a set uniform morality by directly coercive state methods, can thus be none the less seen to possess a dynamic which will implicitly promote some goods while downgrading others' (Stephens 2001a: 7).

I do not propose to comment in detail on either of these strategies for making liberalism more compatible with ecologism. They both have their merits, and to the extent that they succeed they have the capacity to interrupt the flow of the argument (stages (a)–(d), see p. 143) towards the conclusion that the liberal state cannot deliver environmental sustainability. The problem with both strategies, though, is that they involve a full-frontal assault on what many continue to regard as a jewel in liberalism's crown: its commitment to neutrality as far as 'comprehensive doctrines' are concerned. Many of the most cherished items in liberalism's shop window—such as the commitment to toleration—depend, in part at least, on liberal neutrality actually working, in theory and in practice. The tactical disadvantage in the two strategies, then, is that they depend on many modern liberals performing a major volte-face before they can even begin to think about instantiating environmental sustainability. As I indicated at the beginning of the chapter, I propose to offer an alternative account, one which takes the form of an 'immanent critique' of liberal neutrality in order to show that being serious about neutrality involves a more active and normatively self-aware state than we might suspect at first blush. This account allows liberals to remain on their own ground, as it were, but invites them to see that doing so demands a great deal of them in terms of normative commitment.

Let us go back to sustainability for a moment, and specifically to Brian Barry's generic definition of it: 'The core concept of sustainability is, I suggest, that there is some X whose value should be maintained, in as far as it lies within our power to do so, into the indefinite future' (B. Barry 1999: 101). Rather than think of X as any one 'thing', Barry invites us to take the impeccable liberal line of regarding it in terms of opportunities, or 'the chance to live a good life':

it might appear that what should be maintained for future generations is their chance to live a good life as we conceive it. But even if 'we' agreed on what that is (which is manifestly not the case), this would surely be an objectionable criterion for 'what matters'. For one of the defining characteristics of human beings is their ability to form their own conceptions of the good life. It would be presumptuous—and unfair—of us to pre-empt their choices in the future. (This is what is wrong with all utopias). We must respect the creativity of people in the future. What this suggests is that the requirement is to provide future generations with the opportunity to live good lives according to their conception of what constitutes a good life. This should surely include their being able to live good lives according to our conception but should leave other options open to them.

(B. Barry 1999: 103–4)

As Barry points us, there is a liberal and an illiberal version of the provision of opportunities here. The illiberal version is that which focuses on opportunities connected with 'our' (i.e. a determinate) view of the good life, while the liberal version involves a wider set of opportunities—those that will enable future generations to decide which kind(s) of good life they wish to pursue, even if different from our own.

Just what does this provision of equal opportunity across the generations commit the liberal state to? Clearly it must do all it can to prevent the foreclosure of opportunities, and this translates into the commitment to preserve, protect, and otherwise sustain the mental and material wherewithal through which people come to choose, and then live out, their preferred version of the good life. By 'mental wherewithal' I mean the full range of ideas as regards what living the good life might entail.

None of these ideas should be deliberately suppressed—and this is nothing more and nothing less than a commitment to liberal toleration. The additional thought, though, is that liberal neutrality entails the systematic provision and presentation of this full range of ideas. Just as primary schools are encouraged to teach children a full range of religions in religious education classes, so both anthropocentrism and ecocentrism—and cornucopianism—should be offered and examined as reasons for protecting the natural environment (or not). To focus only on one of these would be to stand accused of non-neutrality by omission.

By 'material wherewithal' I mean the environment that provides the physical context through which views of the good life come to be determined, and through which they are enacted. I do not want to get involved in a debate here about 'where ideas come from', but it seems to make prima facie sense to say that the absence of certain types of physical environment could make it impossible to 'think' some versions of the good life, let alone act them out. There is some evidence from recent studies in the science of cognition that bears this out: 'Since categories, schemas and metaphors emerge out of embodied activities, the kinds of possibilities for action that our environments afford become relevant to our understanding of cognition' (Preston 2002: 434). Piers Stephens, too, points in this direction, though in a rather more partisan way: 'if we do indeed need to inculcate virtues of care in relation to the natural, we shall require both a cognitive reorientation and the existence of some nature in our lives to begin with to give an experiential base' (Stephens 2001a: 20). In less partisan terms, if equal opportunity commits the liberal state to providing the fullest possible range of mental or ideological possibilities for its citizens, it is similarly committed to sustaining the fullest possible range of environments via which these possibilities are thought and through which they are lived. A liberal state would therefore be acting illiberally if it allowed the production of a world in which 'people [must] learn to find satisfaction in totally artificial landscapes, walking on the astroturf amid the plastic trees while the electronic birds sing overhead' (B. Barry 1999: 102). And this would be illiberal because it would amount to the foreclosure of routes to thinking and living alternative versions of the good life—versions that involve real birds, real trees, and real grass.

The general idea, then, is to preserve and protect as wide a range of mental and material options as possible. Whether this involves us in preserving and protecting the *favelas* of Brasilia and the slums of Calcutta too is a moot point. I think not, though, on the grounds that these environments are not generally thought of as plausible contexts for living the good life. Less easily disposed of is the suggestion that countries should make every effort to preserve and protect their coal-mining industries, for example, on the grounds that the communities they produce are indeed plausible contexts for the good life. Perhaps this particular example runs up against the objection that mining industries are literally unsustainable in that they rely on a finite resource that will eventually run out. It must be admitted, though, that the general injunction to preserve and protect in the name of liberal neutrality is bound to generate debate over specific candidates for protection and preservation. It must also be admitted that the injunction not to foreclose opportunities is itself a potential foreclosure of opportunities, in that fewer transformations of 'what we already have' seem to be permitted than would otherwise be the case. This may prevent the creation of new products, environments, and social forms that might provide the basis for as yet unthinkable contexts for the good life. It is possible to overstate this point, though, since precaution is not at all a recipe for inaction. The injunction to protect and preserve permits potentially massive transformations within a framework of variety and diversity.

What does all this mean in the specific context of environmental sustainability? What is the X factor? And can liberal societies deliver it? One kind of answer, much favoured by economists, is characterized thus by Bryan Norton: 'what we owe the future should be an opportunity for undiminished utility; and so the question of fairness across generations will be formulated as a comparison of aggregated welfare opportunities available to individuals living at different times' (Norton 1999: 119); or, in an alternative formulation: 'acting sustainably is to avoid causing a reduction in the opportunities of future persons to achieve a level of economic welfare equal to their predecessors' (Norton 1999: 120). On this reading, we are being fair to future generations so long as the opportunities for creating economic welfare do not decrease over time. Note that this stipulation is entirely consistent with Brian Barry's other-world of electronic birds, and plastic trees and grass. There is nothing about such a world that makes it incompatible with very high levels of economic welfare.

It is this that leads Norton to ask a key question: 'Can we make sense of the notion . . . that one might reduce the options available to another person, and thereby harm that person, even while one has protected that person from economic impoverishment?' (Norton 1999: 131). Norton thinks that we can indeed impoverish people at the same time as making them wealthier, and he explains it like this:

suppose that our generation converts all wilderness areas and natural communities into productive mines, farmland, production forests, or shopping centres, and suppose that we do so efficiently, and that we are careful to save a portion of the profits, and invest them wisely, leaving the future far more wealthy than we are. Does it not make sense to claim that, in doing so, we harmed future people, not economically, but in the sense that we seriously and irreversibly narrowed their range of choices and experiences? A whole range of human experience would have been obliterated; the future will have been—at least given the values of many environmentalists—impoverished.

(Norton 1999: 132)

This, to me at least, is powerful and persuasive. But from a liberal point of view Norton undersells his point. For it is not just that the future has been impoverished 'given the values of many environmentalists', but that it has been impoverished in the more general sense of a reduction in the range of options from which future people can choose. In other words, one does not have to be an environmentalist to support Norton's point, one only has to be a liberal who believes that people should be free to choose and to live their versions of the good life. This, in turn, commits the liberal to preserving and protecting—and even promoting—the mental and material preconditions (including the wilderness areas to which Norton refers) for as wide a range of 'good lives' as possible. More to the point, it commits the liberal state to these things too, if it is not to stand accused of non-neutrality by omission.

All this leads Norton to offer an alternative answer to his question of 'what should we save for future generations?' (Norton 1999: 119). It runs as follows:

A second type of answer would proceed not by comparisons of individual well-being, but by listing 'stuff' that should be saved for future generations (the LS approach). By 'stuff' I mean any aspect of the natural world that is physically describable, including important sites, biological taxonomic groups, standing stocks of resources, and important ecological processes. Examples of stuff would include: adequate supplies of fresh, clean water; the Grand Canyon; grizzly bears (or, more generally, 'biological diversity'); an undiminished ozone shield in the upper atmosphere; and also perhaps landscape features, such as a predominantly forested landscape. (Norton 1999: 119)

Alan Holland offers a similar kind of answer:

So far, discussion has focused on natural capital in the sense of the actual and potential economic value residing in natural items. There is, however, another possible approach to the problem of measurement, which is to attempt an inventory of the natural items themselves, and simply rely on 'informed' judgements to decide whether and in what sense there has been any depletion.

(Holland 1999: 63)

Holland's formulation underscores the need to disaggregate when it comes to thinking about sustainability's X factor. Holland and Norton are both opposed to the Lockean view that, from an opportunities point of view, the non-human natural world is best viewed as a repository of potential economic value. It is possible to be opposed to this view for reasons drawn from the politics and philosophy of ecologism—that the non-human natural world has 'intrinsic value', for example. But the liberal defence of a 'listing stuff' approach to what to save for future generations is that it is the best way of cashing out the commitment to neutrality in terms of the good life. To convert all of Locke's 'wast' into productive farmland is to foreclose versions of the good life that depend on apparently empty tracts of land for their articulation and enactment.

We might couch this in terms of the debate between 'weak' and 'strong' sustainability. Weak sustainability is generally taken to describe Norton's first answer to the sustainability question, above: 'acting sustainably is to avoid causing a reduction in the opportunities of future persons to achieve a level of economic welfare equal to their predecessors' (Norton 1999: 120). Supporters of weak sustainability see no need to distinguish between 'human-made' and 'natural' capital, since they believe that the former can always substitute for the latter. There is no need, in other words, to separate out a separate category of 'capital' (let us call it that in this context) and make it a specific object of policies for sustainability. 'Strong' sustainability enthusiasts, on the other hand, do not believe that human-made capital can always substitute for natural capital, and they therefore enjoin us to preserve the latter as a separate intellectual and practical category. Norton neatly summarizes the position as it affects us here as follows: 'We can say, then, that whereas the weak sustainability theorists believe we owe to the future an *unstructured bequest package*, the strong sustainability theorists *structure their bequest package*, differentiating special elements, of capital-in-general that must be included in the capital base passed forward to coming generations' (Norton 1999: 126).

Everything I have said so far suggests that liberals, and the liberal state, should be in favour of strong sustainability—and not because of any special commitment to 'nature', but because a structured bequest package amounts to a wider range of options from which to choose good lives. Strong sustainability is, in other words, a way to maximize neutrality in respect of 'comprehensive doctrines'. The belief in total substitutability found in weak sustainability amounts to a foreclosing of opportunities: you can have any kind of good life you like as long as it is wholly and completely expressible in terms of 'gunk' (or whatever it is into which everything has been converted). Alan Holland makes the following incisive remark, from our point of view, about the 'listing stuff' or strong sustainability approach:

> An initial point to notice is that to adopt such an approach is to do more than adopt a different system of measurement; it is to lay stress on a different kind of value. So far as the measure of economic value is concerned the transformation of a natural item must be seen as enhancing or even creating the natural capital; for it would have no value if it was not utilized or utilizable . . . To focus on the natural items themselves, on the other hand, would seem to involve laying stress on their potential value; and this is not an unreasonable thing . . . To transform them [natural items] is, arguably, to limit the possible range of uses to which they may be put, just as differentiation in the case of the cells limits their developmental role. The 'paradox' of natural capital is that the realization of its potential is at one and the same time the limitation of its potential. (Holland 1999: 63–4)

Transforming natural items, as Holland says, is to limit the range of uses to which they can be put—including the use to which they might be put as sources and expressions of notions of the good life. Piers Stephens is surely right, then, to say that 'a healthy liberalism will encourage the formation of preferences that are authentically the agent's own against a backdrop of the widest possible ranges of potential fulfilment for them to select from' (Stephens 2001*b*: 45–6). In my view this commits liberals and liberal states to something like strong sustainability—a counter-intuitive conclusion, perhaps, given that liberals are usually associated with the neo-classical economic position of weak sustainability.

One of the most widely quoted and evocative ways of outlining the sustainability choices available to us is the following from Marcel Wissenburg:

> We may ... expect the introduction of the notion of limits to growth and resources, and with it that of sustainability, to lead to questions of a substantive normative nature. A sustainable society need not be one big Yellowstone Park—we can imagine a worldwide version of Holland stuffed with cows, grain and greenhouses, or even a global Manhattan without the Park to be as sustainable and for many among us as pleasant as the first. (Wissenburg 1998: 81)

From a practical point of view, any one of these three versions may indeed be sustainable and from an ideological point of view too, in the sense that arguments can be made to show that none of them violates what 'sustainable' might be taken to mean. But from a liberal point of view, elements of all three of them should surely be sustained, since they represent a range of options for the good life that would be reduced if any one of them were to be 'discontinued'. Discontinuation would amount to non-neutrality as far as good lives are concerned. As Stephens says, 'surely a liberal who truly upholds the values of liberty and diversity should opt for whichever model offers the *widest range* of developmental options' (Stephens 2001*a*: 13, emphasis in the original). Norton thus reaches an impeccably liberal conclusion, although he does not describe it as such, when he writes that 'it seems reasonable to think of our obligation to the future as including, in addition to maintaining a fair savings rate, an obligation to maintain a non-diminishing range of choices and opportunities to pursue certain valued interests and activities' (Norton 1999: 132–3). I have to conclude that

Wissenburg is wrong (for once) when he says that 'liberalism fails to support any reason at all for caring about nature' (Wissenburg 2001: 35). This is because, he continues, 'liberalism or at the very least modern liberalism tries not to support any particular theory of the good' (Wissenburg 2001: 35). But it is precisely for this reason that liberalism does have reason to 'care for nature', since if it does not do so it is foreclosing opportunities to envisage and enact good lives that depend on it.

In closing the sequence of thoughts that lead to his conclusion that liberalism offers no reason to care for nature, Wissenburg says that although liberalism tries not to support any particular theory of the good, 'neither does it prohibit it' (Wissenburg 2001: 35). This is a neat expression of the liberal's last redoubt, assailed as s/he often is by the accusation that liberalism entails too anaemic a view of the human condition, devoid of the kinds of totalizing commitments that give meaning to (some) people's lives. I think that as far as sustainability is concerned, liberalism can be much more positive than this. Too often, positions are hedged around with prevarication and precaution, as in the following from Bryan Norton:

who will future people be and how can we identify them? And, how can we know what they will want or need, or what rights they will insist upon? Since individuals who will live in the future cannot express their concerns and interests, and since we are reluctant to impose a particular version of 'the good' upon them, it is difficult even to begin to evaluate policies that will affect them.

(Norton 1999: 124)

Of course it is true that we do not know how future generations will want to live, and if we do see sustainability as about second-guessing what they will want in some determinate way, then we will indeed have a policy evaluation problem. But as we saw Brian Barry say earlier, 'one of the defining characteristics of human beings is their ability to form their own conceptions of the good life. It would be presumptuous—and unfair—of us to pre-empt their choices in the future' (B. Barry 1999: 103–4). Norton's policy evaluation difficulty seems to be based on the assumption that future generations will be living one version of the good life (or at most a very small number of them), and we should somehow 'aim' our policies so as to make that life possible for them. But if we go along with Barry in the belief that,

We must respect the creativity of people in the future [and that] what this suggests is that the requirement is to provide future generations with the opportunity to live good lives according to their conception of what constitutes a good life. This should surely include their being able to live good lives according to our conception but should leave other options open to them.                (B. Barry 1999: 103–4)

If we go along with this, then the specificities of the policy evaluation problem disappear. The issue now is one of making a range of targets available rather than trying to hit any particular one.

So the thoroughgoing liberal will not attempt to judge what future generations will regard as valuable. S/he will therefore reject Norton's assessment that,

The problem...becomes one of specifying those ecological features and processes that support valued future options. On this view, the problem of defining a fair path to the future requires creating a clear articulation of a specific community's long-term values, and of identifying features of the ecosystem and landscape that are essential to maintain these locally important values into the future.
                                        (Norton 1999: 133)

If I am right that the logic of liberal neutrality in respect of the good life pushes liberals towards support for strong forms of sustainability, then it follows that we do not need to think too hard about 'valued future options'. Our task is to ensure the existence of the preconditions for the possibility of choosing between a healthy variety of options, rather than narrowing them down by committing future generations to whatever a present generation happens to regard as 'locally important'.

Of course this injunction still leaves problems. On one reading, it commits us to trying to preserve everything just as it is; only in this way, it might be said, can we fulfil our obligation to hand down a non-declining range of options to the future. From this point of view it is too cavalier of Bryan Norton to say that '[I]f I cut down a mature tree and plant a seedling of the same species, it seems unlikely that I have significantly harmed people of the future' (Norton 1999: 124). What we might call 'irreducible originality' is a potential source of value in the world, and a mature tree could be regarded as an instantiation of such value in certain circumstances. Think of a village green with a yew tree in the middle of it. The yew tree has been there for 200 years, and has become a symbol of village life. The road system around the village green is complex and dangerous, though, and it is proposed to remove the green to make the roads safer. This means removing the yew tree too. The villagers protest that the tree is important to them and they are offered compensation. In effect they are offered a sum of money that the authorities regard as *equivalent* to the symbolic value of the yew tree to the villagers. The villagers say that nothing can compensate for the loss of the tree, so the authorities offer to buy them another yew tree. The villagers protest, again, on the grounds that the new yew tree is not *the same* as the old one. So the authorities propose moving the old one to a new site, instead of chopping it down or replacing it with a new one. Then it turns out that the *site* of the old yew tree was an important part of its value to the villagers, so moving it somewhere else is also unacceptable.

This vignette shows that significant harm can be done unexpectedly, and it also points up the difficult performative territory into which the liberal principle of 'good life' neutrality can take us when it comes to policies for sustainability. A key corollary I want to take forward into Chapter 5 is that if I am right that liberalism's normative neutrality commits it to providing what I have called the 'mental and material wherewithal' for choosing from as wide a range of options for the good life as possible, then the liberal state must surely be an active state. The liberal state can only act as an 'arbitrator' between ways of life (the role that liberal theory usually regards it as performing) if there are extant, viable, and sustainable ways of life from which to choose. In commenting on whether liberal procedural neutrality can ever produce 'green citizens', Marcel Wissenburg writes that: '[T]he most that can be demanded is that people consider arguments for particular green ideologies and respect those living accordingly—and I hope to have given more than enough "formal" reasons for believing that liberalism allows and can even oblige this' (Wissenburg 2001: 37). I would put this more strongly. Liberal neutrality as regards ways of life makes this obligation compulsory rather than optional if it is not to be regarded as illiberal by omission. Again, Wissenburg writes that 'Liberalism is a public philosophy, a code for the public sphere designed to allow individuals to be, say, Buddhists and Aristotelians and hedonists and fruitarians as far as their views about personal salvation are concerned' (Wissenburg 2001: 35). Indeed, and this commits the liberal state to providing the mental and material preconditions for these ways of life—and others—to be practised. In Chapter 5 I discuss what all this means for just one activity, a key one, carried out by the liberal state—the education of its citizens.

# Citizenship, Education, and the Environment

How do people become environmental or ecological citizens? I do not intend to answer this question in full in this chapter, although I shall refer briefly to some suggestive research on the issue towards the end. The route to citizenship on which I shall focus here is through the formal education system, and there are two principal reasons for this. The first is that many countries include a citizenship stream in their formal curricula. It is not always called 'citizenship', but it is there. It did not used to be called 'citizenship' in Britain, for example, but many of the issues one would expect to be treated under this heading were dealt with in cross-curricular fashion under the badge of Personal, Social and Health Education (PSHE). As it happens, as of August 2002, citizenship *is* a compulsory part of the national curriculum in England in secondary (or high) schools. I shall say something about how this happened shortly. The fact that it did happen provides us with an excellent opportunity to study the way in which the environment has been incorporated (or not) into a recently devised citizenship curriculum in a broadly liberal society.

And this is the second reason for looking at the formal educational route to environmental or ecological citizenship. In Chapters 3 and 4 I established the normative nature of both ecological citizenship and the broad objective towards which we might consider the ecological citizen to be working: environmental sustainability. In Chapter 4 I discussed the difficulties this produces for liberal societies whose institutions are generally enjoined to be neutral in respect of the 'good life'. The question, it will be remembered, was this: if sustainability entails a determinate view of the good life, can liberal institutions deliver it? One absolutely key set of institutions is, of course, schools. So the question in this rather more specific case is whether the state school system in such liberal societies can legitimately deliver the stated aim of producing individuals who will work for sustainability and sustainable development. It is probably worth saying in passing that we should distinguish between liberal *individuals* and liberal *institutions*. It is perfectly proper for individuals in a liberal society to hold determinate views of the good life and to try to persuade others of its merits, but the resources of liberal institutions should not be deployed in the service of that version of the good life. Any given teacher, in other words, might cleave to an ecocentric view of environmental sustainability, but s/he should not—on the liberal view—regard the education system as a vehicle for proselytizing and instantiating that view. As Appendix 9 of the Teacher's Guide to the National Curriculum has it: 'The Education Act 1996 aims to ensure that children are not presented with only one side of political or controversial issues by their teachers' (Teachers' Guide—National Curriculum).

## The Context

The idea of environmental or ecological citizenship education brings together two curriculum streams that have traditionally been regarded as separate: education for citizenship, on the one hand, and environmental education (as it is normally called) on the other. (In connection with my previous place of employment, incidentally, I was pleased to read the following: 'Importantly...a decision was made to call a conference on education at the University of Keele in March 1965. It was here that the term "environmental education" was heard for the first time in Britain'; Wheeler 1975: 8.) Although they are hardly ever thought of together, environmental and citizenship education have much in common as far as structural questions regarding their place in the curriculum is concerned. One standard question asked of environmental education, for example, is how it is to be taught. It might, for example, be taught as a separate subject, just as history, mathematics, and geography are taught as separate subjects. On the other hand, given its cross-curricular possibilities, it might be taught *through* these other subjects, in such a way that their environmental content is specifically flagged and discussed. A third possibility is for the 'whole school' to be regarded as the vehicle for environmental education, such that the school's grounds and buildings and the way it is run become a vehicle and a medium for education about the environment.

There is also—inevitably—a 'what?' as well as a 'how?' question. What, in other words, should the curriculum for environmental education contain? The most common way of getting at an answer to this question is by distinguishing between education *about, in,* and *for* the environment. In this nomenclature, education about the environment has to do with understanding the systems and processes at work in the environment—what we would normally think of as the 'scientific' end of environmental education. Education in the environment refers to the distinction between class-based approaches to environmental education and the 'in the field' alternative. Children spied with their teacher in the woods picking up leaves and inspecting fungus are doing their education 'in the environment'. These children are still learning 'about' the environment, of course, and much early environmental education took this form. The implicit question was always *why* these children were learning about the environment, and there was little sense of it having a broader purpose until the idea of education *for* the environment was broached. On this reading, environmental education has the explicit purpose of inculcating frames of mind and habits and practices in pupils that lead to sustainability. The Schools Council Project Environment offered an early intimation of this in 1974:

> most of our teaching about the world around us has been concerned with the collection of factual information. The present emergence of environmental education has come about largely through the need to develop a society which not only understands something about the environment, is aware of the importance of a healthy environment and of the threats to it of irresponsible actions, but which feels a responsibility towards it. As far as schools are concerned the early interest in learning from environment and studies about environment must lead on to a responsibility for environment.
>
> (Schools Council Project Environment 1974: 4)

This view has now been formally endorsed by the British Government: 'Education for sustainable development enables people to develop the knowledge, values and skills to participate in decisions about the way we do things individually and collectively, both locally and globally, that will improve the quality of life now without damaging the planet for the future' (Education for Sustainable Development 1999). The reference to 'knowledge, values and skills' is recognition of a move beyond knowledge-based education 'about' the environment to the value-laden territory of education 'for' sustainability.

Bob Jickling and Helen Spork note the transformative potential of education 'for' the environment, largely absent in the other formulations:

> Undoubtedly these categories [in, about, and for] have been useful and, in particular, the distinction 'education for the environment' has been a valuable idea, helpful in thinking about environmental education. In many contexts, 'education for the environment' has generated powerful images which have resonated with educators seeking empowerment for themselves and their students . . . 'education for the environment' . . . counteracts the tendency of education 'in' and 'about' the environment to reinforce (rather than transform) existing structures and is more likely to liberate 'environmental education' from these tendencies.            (Jickling and Spork 1999: 310)

The very same questions can be—and are—asked of citizenship education, and schools in England are currently grappling with the best way of meeting their statutory obligation to teach citizenship. Similar types of answer to the 'how?' question are offered: as a single subject, through other subjects, via the whole school. As for what is to be taught, the specific details of citizenship and environmental education curricula are inevitably different, but the structural issues are interestingly similar. This is to say that just as environmental education has moved on from the acquisition of knowledge to the negotiation of values, so citizenship education is no longer only about learning how parliament functions, but has also to do with the moral and ethical dimension of social life. We might say, in other words, that just as environmental education now includes but goes beyond 'environmental literacy', so citizenship education now includes but goes beyond 'political literacy'.

So despite the fact that environmental education and education for citizenship have developed along separate paths, the questions that animate them, and the potential answers to those questions, have strikingly similar characteristics. As I indicated above there is one final question that particularly interests me: the question of what kind of education can legitimately take place in a broadly liberal system of education. I posed this question in the context of education for environmental or ecological citizenship (where citizenship and environmental education are already combined, as it were), but it is clear that this question has dogged citizenship and environmental education separately. In the context of citizenship there has always been the fear that education 'could leave schools and their pupils open to political manipulation and indoctrination' (Arthur and Wright 2001: 72). In the more specific context of liberal societies, Will Kymlicka writes that: 'Even the most minimal conception of liberal citizenship, therefore, requires a significant range of civic virtues. But are schools the appropriate arena to teach these virtues, given that this would involve inculcating substantive (and controversial) moral beliefs?' (1999: 85). These concerns are, as I say, paralleled in discussions about environmental education, particularly where this is understood to refer to education *for* the environment. Jickling and Spork, for example, ask 'Should education aim to advance particular ends, such as red-green environmentalism or sustainable development?, and is it the job of education to make people think, believe or behave in a particular way?' (Jickling and Spork 1999: 312).

To summarize so far, then, we have three questions, an answer to each of which is a necessary condition for determining whether environmental or ecological citizenship education can be effectively delivered in liberal societies. (Let me stress that answers to these questions are not a sufficient condition for determining larger questions such as (a) whether ecological citizenship is possible in liberal societies more generally, or (b) whether ecological citizenship can contribute to environmental sustainability.) The three questions are: what is to be taught, how is it to be taught, and can it be legitimately taught in a liberal education system. I propose to offer answers to these questions by examining the case of the new citizenship curriculum in England that, as I said, became a statutory obligation for secondary schools in August 2002.

## Citizenship Education in England

The statutory presence of citizenship in the secondary school curriculum came about, briefly, as follows. Almost immediately after the election of the first New Labour administration in 1997, the then Secretary of State for Education and Employment, David Blunkett, pledged to 'strengthen education for citizenship and the teaching of democracy in schools' (Qualifications and Curriculum Authority 1998: 4). David Kerr has provided a succinct summary of why this was deemed necessary:

Firstly, the social, political and moral fabric of society in England has seemingly been eroded by the impact of rapid economic and social change. This has resulted in increasing disquiet in many quarters, at the apparent breakdown of the institutions and values that have traditionally underpinned society and encouraged social cohesion and stability, such as marriage, family and respect for the law. There has been particular concern about growing apathy towards public life and participation, as evidenced at the formal level by the decline in the number of people voting at national, local and European elections. Secondly, such developments have had an apparently damaging effect on contemporary English society. A number of research studies, both national and comparative, have concluded that there is a perceptible decline in civic culture in English society, in contrast to other countries, and a marked absence of a political and moral discourse in public life. (Kerr 2001: 8)

Blunkett set up an Advisory Group with the following terms of reference: 'to provide advice on effective education for citizenship in schools—to include the nature and practices of participation in democracy; the duties, responsibilities and rights of individuals as citizens; and the value to individuals and society of community activity'. The Chair of the Advisory Group was Blunkett's former university tutor, political scientist Professor Bernard Crick, and his team duly produced a report, 'Education for Citizenship and the Teaching of Democracy in Schools', in 1998. The main conclusion and recommendation ran as follows: 'We unanimously advise the Secretary of State that citizenship and the teaching of democracy, construed in a broad sense that we will define, is so important both for schools and the life of the nation that there must be a statutory requirement on schools to ensure that it is part of the entitlement of all pupils' (Qualifications and Curriculum Authority 1998: 7). And so education for citizenship as part of the national curriculum for 11–16-year-olds was born, and students across this age range began to be taught it from September 2002.

The aim is nothing other than a sea change in young people's understanding of, and involvement in, political and social issues. As Bernard Crick himself has put it:

We aim at no less than a change in the political culture of this country both nationally and locally; for people to think of themselves as active citizens, willing, able and equipped to have an influence in public life and with critical capacities to weigh evidence before speaking and acting; to build on and to extend radically to young people the best in existing traditions of community involvement and public service, and to make them individually confident in finding new forms of involvement and action among themselves. There are worrying levels of apathy, ignorance and cynicism about public life. These, unless tackled at every level, could well diminish the hoped for benefits both of constitutional reform and of the changing nature of the welfare state.

(B. Crick in Arthur and Wright 2001: 18)

Ambitious indeed. It is far too early to say at present whether this effort will make a difference to levels of apathy and involvement in what we might call 'official' politics (I draw the contrast because it might simply be that young people construe their politics, and do it in a different way, to Crick and his type and generation), but a target has been set, together with a means for tracking progress: 'the DfES [Department for Education and Skills] has funded a seven-year study to see if this September's [2002] 11-year-olds will, by 18, know more about the political, economic, social and voluntary institutions of this country and will be more involved in community and voluntary work than at present. If the results are negative or inconclusive, then compulsion [of citizenship teaching] should be ended' (Crick 2002: 19).

The presence of citizenship in the national curriculum obviously offers the prima facie possibility of environmental and/or ecological citizenship being taught too. Whether it is, and whether it has a chance of being successful, depends at least in part on appropriate answers to the three questions I outlined earlier: what is to be taught, how is it to be taught, and can it be legitimately taught in a liberal education system? As for the first question, The Citizenship Order is very unprescriptive in its detail; the intention is 'light touch' and the methods of delivering the broadly defined content of the syllabus, in particular, are left up to individual schools to decide. There is, though, sufficient information in the National Curriculum guidelines, and in the cross references between these guidelines and other specific subjects, such as geography, history, and English, to form a judgement as to the extent to which environmental and ecological dimensions could be a part of the generic citizenship curriculum.

## What is to be Taught?

Distilling aspects of Chapters 2 and 3, we can develop a rough-and-ready template for a citizenship curriculum in the environmental context. Our exploration of *environmental* citizenship pointed up the importance of rights, so any curriculum that fails to broach this question will be incomplete. Second, justice is a key component of *ecological* citizenship, with an explicitly transnational and duty- or responsibility-oriented component. Citizenship curricula must therefore raise the issue of international, and perhaps intergenerational, and even interspecies, obligations. Similarly, I made it plain in Chapter 4 that I consider sustainable development to be at least as much about values as about techniques and technologies. Science might be able to tell us what the threshold tolerances of nitrogen in the atmosphere are for any given species, but it cannot tell us which species we should be concerned about. The key questions, then, are not technical—they are *normative*. Bearing this in mind, we have to say that we will be short-changed by any ecological citizenship curriculum that does not confront normative questions of this sort.

For those accustomed to thinking of citizenship education in terms of 'civics' courses that focus on the mechanics, structures, and processes of the political system, this list of desiderata, although brief, will already be a bridge too far. The most that a traditional civics course is likely to produce is an awareness of constitutional environmental rights (where they exist), and it might just, therefore, provide a toehold on what I have called environmental citizenship. Civics courses nearly always understand citizenship in the territorial way I associated with liberal and civic republican citizenship in Chapter 2, and are therefore unlikely to take on the international and intergenerational challenges that I regard as a hallmark of post-cosmopolitan—and, by extension, ecological—citizenship. The civics focus on a descriptive mechanics of the political system has also tended to exclude systematic attention to normative questions and how to negotiate them. This makes such courses absolutely unsuited to confronting the normative dilemmas associated with ecological citizenship.

Given all this, it is encouraging to find an explicit rejection, in the English case, of the civics approach to teaching citizenship. Bernard Crick puts it like this:

We have tried to construct a curriculum that will not bore the kids, as old-fashioned civics did. Rather than learning facts about institutions, it encourages discussion of "events, issues and problems" and suggests that pupils learn about institutions best when they have to know how to get something done. They are to be given opportunities for group activities both in school and the community.          (Crick 2002: 17)

The intention is to avoid the old civics centre of gravity, 'with its emphasis on pupils' acquisition of knowledge and understanding of national history and the structures and processes of government and political life', and to focus, instead, on 'equipping pupils with a set of tools (knowledge and understanding, skills and aptitudes, values and dispositions, and key concepts) which prepare them for active and informed participation in their roles, responsibilities and duties in adult life' (Kerr 2001: 10). The view that citizenship is to be regarded at least as much a matter of political theory as of political institutions is cemented when we see Crick referring to 'words like rights and duties, responsibilities, tolerance, freedom and understanding diversity' as the stuff of citizenship (Crick 2002: 17).

So far so good, perhaps, at least as far as a framework for teaching ecological citizenship is concerned. But what about the more specific environmental and ecological content of the citizenship curriculum? Is there any? Once again the signs are good. The curriculum asks specifically for:

education for sustainable development, through developing pupils' skills in, and commitment to, effective participation in the democratic and other decision-making processes that affect the quality, structure and health of environments and society and exploring values that determine people's actions within society, the economy and the environment.

(Department for Education and Employment and
the Qualifications and Curriculum Authority: 8)

This reference to 'sustainable development' opens the door to a systematic exploration of the relationship between this objective and citizenship. One fear, though, might be that sustainable development education will be delivered as a series of largely technical moves. As I pointed out above, though, there is a welcome determination, though, in both the Crick Report and in the curriculum guidelines, to avoid teaching citizenship as if it were a matter of learning the institutional nuts and bolts of politics. Our template, earlier, contained reference to norms and values, so it is encouraging to see the curriculum containing the instruction to teach: 'spiritual development, through fostering pupils' awareness and understanding of meaning and purpose in life and of differing values in human society' (Department for Education and Employment and the Qualifications and Curriculum Authority: 7). This may seem a rather grandiose objective, and citizenship purists may feel it goes way beyond the classical remit of rights and responsibilities to the constituted political authority. I believe, though, that it provides a helpful statutory context within which to teach ecological citizenship, precisely because it contains the injunction to learn about, and negotiate, questions of value. Indeed specific reference to the value-laden content of sustainable development is made in the Teachers' Guide to the National Curriculum: 'Pupils...explore the values that underpin the actions of individuals and communities and how these affect the environment, the economy and society' (Teachers' Guide 2002). Again, 'Citizenship provides specific opportunities for pupils to explore the range of attitudes and values in society and *to consider the kind of society they want to live in*' (Teachers' Guide 2002; emphasis added). The emphasized part of this formulation provides an excellent opportunity—for the teacher who wishes to grasp it—to broach key questions at the heart of sustainability and sustainable development, and therefore at the core of what it might mean to be an ecological citizen. The classic sustainability conundrum is: what kind of a world do we want to pass on to future generations? This raises questions of value related to environmental protection: do we want Blade Runner or The Waltons? Or something else entirely? Is it possible that future generations will want electronic birds and plastic trees? Are we enjoined, as a matter of justice, to provide the wherewithal for them? And so on.

All this is underscored by the requirement to teach 'moral development, through helping pupils develop a critical appreciation of issues of right and wrong, justice, fairness, rights and obligations in society' (Department for Education and Employment and the Qualifications and Curriculum Authority: 7). The triumvirate of 'justice, fairness and obligation' is particularly important given everything I have said about environmental and ecological citizenship being underpinned by notions of justice. The presence of the triumvirate indicates that a key part of the curricular framework is in place for these types of citizenship to bulk large in secondary school citizenship education in England. This is especially the case if we add in the references to values, noted above, which are such a crucial element in determining what sustainability might be.

I would sound one cautionary note, though, in regard to the way in which 'community service' is often regarded as a laudable component of citizenship curricula—particularly in the context of encouraging an 'active' sense of citizenship. A typical expression of this runs as follows:

The aim of community involvement as a dimension of citizenship education is linked with pupils learning the meaning of social interdependence and democratic principles. Every pupil's education should include experiential learning of the kind offered by community service. Again many consider it to be an indispensable prerequisite of citizenship education and cite many benefits for it. Few English schools organise any sustained or integrated community service experiences for their pupils. (Arthur and Wright 2001: 13)

Visiting old people's homes, putting out their rubbish bins, erasing graffiti, and tidying grass verges—all these are plausible aspects of a very broad conception of citizenship, but none of them are explicitly founded in justice. From this more specifically political point of view, I would prefer to see the active and participatory aspects of citizenship education take place in campaigning contexts where questions of justice are explicitly at stake. I shall say something more about this towards the end of the chapter.

These last remarks connect with another key element in ecological citizenship—its irreducibly transnational dimension; ecological footprints cannot be confined to national boundaries. As I pointed out in Chapter 2, citizenship denotes a relationship between strangers and it is crucial that it be distinguished from neighbourliness in the minds of pupils. I think, therefore, that the following injunction is insufficient: 'Children should learn from the very beginning self-confidence and socially and morally responsible behaviour both in and beyond the classroom, both towards those in authority and towards each other' (Kerr 2001: 14). In this context, in contrast, it is encouraging to see the curricular obligation to learn about 'the work of community-based, national and international voluntary groups... the importance of resolving conflict fairly... the world as a global community, and the political, economic, environmental and social implications of this, and the role of the European Union, the Commonwealth and the United Nations' (Department for Education and Employment and the Qualifications and Curriculum Authority: 14). This is a welcome move beyond the territorial conception of citizenship that confines us to liberal and civic republican understandings of the issue. The door is opened to cosmopolitan and post-cosmopolitan treatments and therefore, specifically, to ecological citizenship which has non-territoriality at its heart. Students are encouraged to see that: 'There is a global dimension to the jobs we do, the clothes we wear, the food we eat, the music we listen to' (Teachers' Guide 2002). There is even the possibility of a spot of direct action, since the curriculum at Key Stage 4 (age 15–16) requires that pupils be taught 'the opportunities for individuals and voluntary groups to bring about social change locally, nationally, in Europe, and internationally' (Department for Education and Employment and the Qualifications and Curriculum Authority: 15).

I pointed out at the beginning of the chapter that the idea of environmental or ecological citizenship education brings together two themes in the curriculum that have hitherto been largely separated: citizenship and environmental education. Happily, from the point of view of an effective framework for teaching ecological citizenship (in particular, and as distinct from environmental citizenship), developments have taken place in both these themes that mean that base camp has been reached. By this I mean that the normative content of both themes has been recognized and that there is therefore a greater likelihood of ecological citizenship being taught, and being taught effectively, than would otherwise have been the case.

As I pointed out earlier, the move beyond 'political literacy' in citizenship education has been paralleled by a move beyond 'environmental literacy' in environmental education. This makes for a promising panorama of opportunities when the two are brought together in the guise of what I want to call ecological citizenship. Bernard Crick's Advisory Group on citizenship identified three elements in citizenship teaching: 'social and moral responsibility', 'community involvement', 'political literacy' (in Kerr 2001: 14). In the old civics courses, most likely only the last of these would have appeared. Similarly in the environmental context Steve Goodall points out that:

education about the environment, its climate, geology, water, resources, living systems and human activities can only provide a common framework within which the moral and values debate takes place. One cannot teach about the environment without ascribing values to the existence and desirability of certain kinds of environment. Pupils may debate how to ensure the best immediate and future use of the environment. They may consider possible solutions to environmental problems taking into account conflicting interests and making informed choices. In doing so they are taking part in a moral and political debate.
(Goodall 1994: 5–6)

As far as the question of what is to be taught in the citizenship curriculum in England, then, the framework provides a promising basis for the teaching of ecological citizenship. At worst, the possibility of teaching it is not excluded, and at best, the normative aspects of the syllabus, as well as some of the more specific and substantive guidelines in it, actually encourage it. Whether it will be taught, though, and how effectively, will depend on a host of structural and quotidian factors in individual schools. Among the former, there is the question of how it is to be taught, and it is to this I now turn.

## How is it to be Taught?

For present purposes I take this question to refer to the place of environmental or ecological citizenship education in the curriculum. 'How?' might also be taken to refer to the method of teaching, of course, and answers might include 'text-based classroom learning', or 'activity-based learning through campaigns', or both. I shall refer to this understanding of the question from time to time but it will not be the central focus of this section.

As far as the curriculum is concerned, then, I introduced the question near the beginning of the chapter by pointing out that potential answers to it are common to both citizenship and environmental education theory. The three answers most commonly given are that such education might be delivered as a single subject, through other subjects in the curriculum, and as a 'whole school' enterprise. In what follows I shall discuss these three standard options, and then suggest a fourth, more novel, one. Up to now, in the United Kingdom at least, both citizenship and environmental education have been regarded as 'cross-curricular' subjects. Their presence in and relevance to all subjects is thereby recognized, but the theoretical importance granted to them has rarely been reflected in education practice. The statutory demands of teaching assessable core subjects has usually crowded out the possibility of the effective cross-curricular teaching of citizenship and the environment.

It was recognition of this, indeed, that led Bernard Crick and his Advisory Committee on Citizenship to recommend that citizenship have its own statutory (and compulsorily assessable) place in the curriculum. On the face of it this marks a shift from teaching citizenship 'through other subjects' to teaching it in its own right. This is indeed a possibility, but the 'citizenship through subject' approach still bulks large. As Arthur and Wright point out:

Although all subjects of the curriculum will be expected to contribute to the teaching of citizenship, English, history and geography in particular have been singled out as providing a distinctive contribution to its promotion...As a result, aspects of the Citizenship Order have been inserted into the individual programmes of study for English, history and geography and will in effect form part of them. These 'citizenship insertions' will ensure that the content of some lessons in the subject is guided to comply with the imperatives of the Citizenship Order. What this means in practice is effectively a 'two-birds-with-one-stone' approach: when addressing the nature of the Stalinist state in the Soviet Union, or the Holocaust, for example, teachers will simultaneously be addressing and emphasising the need stated in the Citizenship Order to teach the 'legal and human rights and responsibilities underpinning society'. (Arthur and Wright 2001: 29–30)

*Mutatis mutandis*, precisely the same kinds of opportunities exist in the context of environmental and ecological citizenship education. Ros McCulloch points out, for example, that 'The contribution of English to environmental awareness might start...by introducing pupils to poems and stories in the English canon that emphasise personal responsibility for the natural world' (McCulloch 1994: 43–4). David Cain argues that 'Environmental problem-solving is clearly one area where there is vast scope for mathematical activity. A task such as creating a garden, a pond or a reserve for wild life will require the use of the kind of skills which should already be developing under the heading of "Using and Applying Mathematics"' (Cain 1994: 49). Tina Jarvis holds out the following kind of possibility in the context of Design and Technology:

Other conflicts can be explored by designing a zoo. Pupils will have to choose between the demands of the public to see animals clearly, and the needs of the animals for a suitable environment. They may balance taking animals from their natural environment and the need to educate people to care for animals. Conservation of the ecological balance in natural environments may be weighed against improving the breeding rate of rare animals. (Jarvis 1994: 58)

Even Finance classes turn out to be a possible context for environmental (citizenship) education:

Allowing for the following costs one must question whether recycling glass bottles, by even the most modern methods, is cost-effective:

—fuel used going to the bottlebank;
—manufacture of the skip;
—rent of space for the skip;
—lorry to collect the skip;
—energy to melt the glass;
—occasional quality rejects. (Duffell 1994: 106–7)

These brief vignettes illustrate the authentic scope that exists for 'teaching the environment' through other curricular subjects. This is formally recognized, indeed, in the cross-curricular advice given to teachers in the citizenship curriculum. Geography is continually cross-referenced. Under 'Knowledge and understanding of places', for example, students are invited 'to explain how places are interdependent [for example, through trade, aid, international tourism, acid rain], and to explore the idea of global citizenship'. A note remarks that 'These develop pupils' understanding of global citizenship, which includes awareness of what it means to be a citizen in the local community and of the United Kingdom, Europe and the wider world' (http://www.nc.uk.net/nc/contents/Gg-3–POS.html).

This approach to teaching both citizenship and the environment has its pitfalls, however. At its most general level, Arthur and Wright point out that the cross-curricular teaching of citizenship:

> was characterised by a number of hallmarks which suggested that it had failed to address the problems it had been introduced to resolve. Among these were found the following: it was a non-assessment pursuit which had been taught largely by non-specialist teachers and delivered through personal and social education; its content was seldom made explicit and teachers were often left to divine it from what had been implied; there was also a lack of consistency in provision, with, at the more negative end, resistance to it from subject staff and little use being made of the wider community; it was found that such a lack of enthusiasm had filtered down to the pupils who viewed it as a low-status endeavour which had to be endured rather than enjoyed; the end 'result' was that pupils were unable to understand the connections between citizenship and their own individual subject, or indeed, more general aspects of the curriculum. The situation was bleak for citizenship education in many schools as it had relied upon being integrated into existing subjects of the curriculum, but this clearly had not been effective.          (Arthur and Wright 2001: 22)

Making it a statutory requirement to teach citizenship, and making it assessable, is supposed to help overcome these difficulties—and it may indeed do so, although there is of course no evidence one way or another at present. My anecdotal evidence, for what it is worth, suggests that the assessable nature of citizenship is indeed concentrating minds, that Postgraduate Certificate of Education courses will produce some specialist citizenship teachers, that the citizenship curriculum guidelines have helped teachers decide what needs to be taught, but that provision is patchy—and may continue to be for some time.

There is still the sense of citizenship as an optional extra, to be covered when all the other important subjects are done and dusted. Ian Potter's advice on 'implementing citizenship education' is worrying: 'Our advice would be to identify what, in the orders, is already being "covered". The extent to which the requirements of citizenship education are currently in place probably won't be a surprise. What will be a pleasant discovery is the likelihood that little will in fact need to be implemented' (Potter 2001: 48). Even the architect of the citizenship curriculum, Bernard Crick, seems sometimes to fall into this 'line of least resistance' trap. Debating with the Conservative Party's 'shadow' secretary of state for education and skills, Damian Green, Crick responded to Green's concern that citizenship would overload already busy teachers with this response: 'The guidance on teaching citizenship (from the Qualifications and Curriculum Authority) says that while a school may choose to deliver it as a separate subject, most of it can be delivered through other subjects with only minor adjustments' (Crick 2002: 16).

This seems insufficient to produce the systematic attention to citizenship that Crick wants. Arthur and Wright are surely correct in saying that we 'need to recognise that it is almost impossible for any one subject to cover all that is required in teaching citizenship education' (2001: 21), despite Crick saying that 'My personal view, that I have had to be a little bit discreet about at times, is that of all the other subjects History may have (should have) overall the greatest role to play' (Crick 2001: p. xix). In practice, schools are likely to choose a combination of the three standard options for 'delivering' citizenship education, and these same three options are relevant to its environmental component. First, environmental or ecological citizenship can and should be taught through all subjects because:

environmental concerns touch every area of life and so are relevant to all subjects. Environmental studies can appear as a branch of geography.

But when secondary school pupils learn about atomic physics, about economics, about biological systems and about the industrial synthesis of organic chemicals, they should also be taught about nuclear waste, about environmental cost-benefit analysis, about population dynamics and about techniques of clean production.

(Taylor 1992: 99)

Second, the fact that citizenship has its own place in the timetable, combined with the presence of sustainability issues (already noted) in the citizenship curriculum, can only help to raise the profile of environmental and ecological citizenship. And third, engaging the whole school, as an institution, in working out the meaning and practice of such citizenship is a means of signalling and cementing its importance in the minds of pupils and staff alike.

I said earlier that I would suggest a fourth approach to teaching both citizenship and environmental education, so let me close this section with a sketch of this possibility. My remarks so far in this chapter point to the conclusion that the requirements of the English citizenship curriculum are pretty well suited to teaching the specific cases of environmental and ecological citizenship—contrary to what one might expect from a citizenship curriculum, given its likely institutional orientation. But we might go further. A case could be made that the entire curriculum be taught *through* these citizenships, because practically every theme in the curriculum is importantly present in them. So, for example, the injunction to help pupils 'develop a critical appreciation of... rights and obligations in society' (Department for Education and Employment and the Qualifications and Curriculum Authority 1999: 7) could be fully met through an examination of the difference between environmental and ecological citizenship, explained in Chapter 3. The former is a rights-based conception of the relationship between citizenship and the environment, while the latter picks up the obligations tradition of civic republican citizenship and takes it into the global environmental arena.

Similarly, two other aspects of the 'moral development' part of the citizenship curriculum—'justice and fairness'—lie at the very heart of ecological citizenship, so a curriculum organized 'through the environment' would provide ample and concrete opportunity to deal with them. We know that the key sustainability question is 'what kind of world do we want to hand on to future generations?', so this provides a perfect platform to 'foster pupils' awareness and understanding of meaning and purpose in life and of differing values in human society', as the curriculum enjoins teachers to do. Likewise, it is not hard to imagine how environmental issues in any given school's community would provide the opportunity for pupils to 'share ideas, formulate policies and take part in responsible action in communities'. Indeed 'the environment' is an exemplary vehicle for the deployment of all the so-called 'key skills' in the citizenship curriculum: communication, application of number (use and abuse of statistics), IT, and problem solving. The 'political literacy' parts of the curriculum cry out for a case-based treatment so as to avoid the dangers of desiccation present in anything that sounds like the old civics courses. What better than an environmental dispute (e.g. plans for a bypass) to pick over the 'characteristics of parliamentary and other forms of government', the work of 'community-based voluntary groups', 'how the economy functions', 'the importance of resolving conflict fairly', and 'the importance of playing an active part in democratic and electoral processes'? Finally, I have already pointed out how key internationalist themes in ecological citizenship provide an ideal opportunity to broach other curriculum issues such as 'the world as a global community', and 'global interdependence and responsibility'. In sum, then, the curriculum injunction to teach 'education for sustainable development' might profitably be regarded as a vehicle for teaching the citizenship curriculum as a whole—an alternative option to the three I discussed earlier.

## Liberal Impartiality

The general question that has animated this chapter is whether environmental and ecological citizenship can be effectively delivered in liberal societies. I suggested that this general question can best be answered through three contributory sub-questions, the last of which was whether a liberal education system—committed to neutrality as far as 'plans for life' are concerned—can cope with the value-laden nature of sustainability questions. I have offered positive answers to the first two questions, at least as far as this case study of the English citizenship curriculum is concerned. It remains, then, to confront the last one.

Liberals have long been suspicious of citizenship and citizenship education because these 'are highly contested concepts. Historically, they have been appropriated by politicians and educators at every point in the political spectrum, to promote local, regional, national, international or global agendas, and social, cultural, political or commercial interests' (Moss 2001: p. xiii). More specifically, in a formulation to which I referred earlier in the chapter, Arthur and Wright say that 'With a central government-sponsored Citizenship Order some believe that this could leave schools and their pupils open to political manipulation and indoctrination' (2001: 72). 'Indoctrination', they continue, 'is a difficult and complex area with a variety of meanings in the literature. It essentially means that a teacher teaches something as true regardless of evidence and their pupils accept it unquestionably' (2001: 76). Most of us, teachers included, have points of view, and the following way of dealing with them in the school context seems unimpeachable: 'Bias is something that few of us, if any, are free from and while it is legitimate and entirely natural for teachers to have their own commitments it cannot be acceptable for them to teach in a biased way' (Arthur and Wright 2001: 76).

# Citizenship, Education, and the Environment

But might there not be reasons for teaching in a 'biased way' that trump this commitment to a thoroughgoing neutrality? As Arthur and Wright themselves go on to say, 'It may however, be legitimate for them [teachers] to teach in a committed way in order to change some individual attitudes in the classroom—such as racist or sexist remarks' (2001: 76). Most liberals will agree with this suggestion, and some of them may even concur with the implications of the view that liberalism harbours its own set of values with which pupils need inculcating: 'liberal democracy...is not neutral and expects teachers to promote procedural values which includes applying democratic principles within the community, beginning in the classroom' (Arthur and Wright 2001: 76). Will Kymlicka makes a similar point:

Liberal citizenship requires cultivating the habit of civility, and the capacity for public reasonableness, in our interaction with others. Indeed, it is precisely these habits and capacities that most need to be learned in schools, for they are unlikely to be learned in smaller groups or associations, like the family, neighbourhood or church, which tend to be homogeneous in their ethnocultural backgrounds and religious beliefs. (Kymlicka 1999: 88)

There seems to be room, therefore, for some rather determinate substantive and procedural values to be taught in a liberal education system. Maybe this dawning recognition is why, perhaps surprisingly, after Bernard Crick's Advisory Group's initial report and recommendations on the teaching of citizenship, 'There was...little public or professional concern expressed about the dangers of political indoctrination of pupils, a factor which has dogged discussion of citizenship education in the past' (Kerr 2001: 18; for a characteristically idiosyncratic exception, though, see Flew 2000).

Now, as we saw in Chapter 4, it has been suggested that the objective of environmental sustainability entails living a determinate kind of 'good life'. If ecological citizenship is about living this life, then many will say that it cannot be legitimately taught in liberal education systems because of the liberal commitment to state neutrality. Is this view undermined, though, by the 'new realism' repres-ented by Kymlicka and others regarding the positive desirability of inculcating some determinate habits, practices, and values in liberal citizens? Well it might—if it were true that environmental sustainability involved living a deter-minate type of good life; if, in other words, 'truth' and 'falsity' were categories appropriate to the discourse and practice of sustainability. Much of Chapter 4 was devoted to showing, however, that they are not. Environmental sustainability, as dis-course and as practice, is always under construction. As such, as I argued in Chapter 4, the appropriate liberal commitment is not to offer some determinate account of it, but to ensure the condi-tions within which the widest range of opportunities for think-ing and living sustainability are authentically available.

In the context of environmental and ecological citizenship education, then, 'bias' is much more likely to occur through the *omission* of views regarding the sustainable good life than by the unexamined proselytizing of one version of it by any individual teacher (although there will of course be occasions when these amount to the same thing). This is the educational analogue of the point I made in the previous chapter regarding 'weak' and 'strong' sustainability. Weak sustainability reduces the different-iated 'stuff' of nature to its lowest common denominator as a source of economic welfare. Strong sustainability, on the other hand, insists that human-made capital cannot always substi-tute for natural capital, in part because each category is a source of mental and material inspiration for different views of the good life. Liberals should commit to strong sustainability, there-fore, not on the basis that there are 'values in nature', but because it is the best way of achieving neutrality as far as 'com-prehensive doctrines' are concerned. Similarly, liberal neutral-ity in education demands that the citizenship syllabus enable and encourage the teaching of the widest possible range of meanings and practices of environmental sustainability. The guidance in the British Government's Education Act of 1996 is such that 'If schools do not ensure that their pupils are offered a balanced presentation of opposing views when teaching controversial issues then anyone can make a formal complaint under the legislation' (Arthur and Wright 2001: 82). This is usually taken to refer to the undiluted and systematic *presence* of one point of view. In our present context we need to see that neutrality can also be threatened by the *absence* of points of view.

I can illustrate this point by referring briefly to a lesson plan designed to introduce the ideas of population growth to Key Stage 1 children, introduced without further comment by Joy Palmer and Philip Neal as follows:

Equipment: clear plastic box and enough marbles for the box to overflow.

Strategy:

1 Explain that the box is the classroom and the children must put one marble in for each child in the class.

2 Explain that hypothetically in 50 years' time, the class could have twice as many children if the population grows too much. Put into the box the right number of marbles to double the class.

3 As the box overflows, talk about how there would not be enough room for everyone, not enough chairs, paint, pencils, etc.

4 Discuss how this relates to the developing world and people's lack of food and water if the population continues growing at a high rate.

(Palmer and Neal 1994: 58)

The flaw in this plan is that it fails to enable debate between the merits of what adults might call 'cornucopian' and 'sufficiency' ways of living. Resource use is not only a function of raw population numbers but also of per capita consumption. At the very least, therefore, Palmer and Neal's children should be offered some large and some small marbles, to illustrate the differential per capita consumption rates of 'average' Americans and Bangladeshis, say. Note that by no stretch of the imagination can the designer of this lesson plan be accused of 'bias' or 'indoctrination' in the normal senses of these words. It is rather the omission of a key factor in the debate that stymies the possibility of the 'balanced presentation of opposing views' enjoined by the Education Act. This, then, is an example of 'non-neutrality by omission'.

So a liberal education system must commit to teaching a full range of views regarding the sustainable good life, and it must embrace the ambiguities, tensions, and contradictions present in the sustainability injunction. Michael Bonnet rightly says that ' "sustainable development" is a highly problematic term, open to a variety of interpretations and arguably also subject to internal contradictions. These clearly need to be addressed if the concept is to serve a constructive function in our understanding of environmental policy and, equally, such clarification is necessary to examining the possibility of education for sustainable development' (Bonnet 2002: 9). It would be a mistake, though, to take 'addressing and clarifying' contradictions to mean trying to establish the 'truth' of sustainable development, since there isn't one. I would rather take 'addressing and clarifying' to refer to the process of moral reasoning that enables people to make informed choices about the right kind of life to lead. Once again let me stress that a precondition for this is a full range of 'kinds of life' from which to choose. This seems quite uncontroversially compatible with liberal intentions, if hardly ever systematically present in practice.

But a second precondition may be more disputable from a liberal point of view. This is the requirement that pupils be explicitly confronted with 'true believers'. David Carr distinguishes between a conservative and a liberal view of education with this: 'the problem in question is not so much that of how to live, but that of how to let live' (Carr 1999: 33). He glosses this as follows:

These new liberal educationalists saw the principal aim of education as basically that of the promotion of personal autonomy; on this view, education and schooling ought to be concerned with equipping individuals with the rational resources to decide for themselves how they should live, who they should be, what goals to pursue, what to produce, what to consume and so on. All else—any attempt to influence individuals in some particular direction or to determine in advance their spiritual, social or economic destiny—could only count as just so much unacceptable indoctrination or coercion.          (Carr 1999: 32)

But this is surely a false dichotomy. I suspect it is true that it 'is only by being initiated into some form of moral life that individuals are in a position to make judgements or express opinions about what is moral' (Crittenden 1999: 58). 'Moral reasoning' is not only a matter, therefore, of deploying what Ruth Jonathan felicitously calls the ' "look no hands" procedural principles of liberal moral education' (Jonathan 1999: 75), but of confronting students with live examples of commitment. On this reading it is a requirement for teachers to say not only 'here is a view' but also 'I hold that view'. At this point moral reasoning can get going. So I would endorse Jonathan's view that:

to develop in the young the capacity for critical reflection on values cannot in and of itself provide an adequate framework either for the development of individual commitments or for the shared social understandings that both shape and reflect those commitments. Indeed, the rationale for such reflection in individuals presupposes the existence of a surrounding framework of value that both supports and sustains, and against which personal values are elaborated and modified.                    (Jonathan 1999: 64–5)

This runs counter to the notion that the best way of teaching people how to negotiate values is through 'the idea of the "impartial chairperson" by which the teacher avoids stating his or her own position and keeps to procedural rules—in effect the teacher renounces their authority as "expert" ' (Arthur and Wright 2001: 76). Not only does the 'impartial chairperson' embody and express the values of liberal 'procedural "one-club golfing" ' (Jonathan 1999: 74), but the position can only be occupied by someone (on any intelligible definition of impartiality) in possession of all the facts and values available— also known as an expert. As the Schools Council Project Environment put it:

> There is a good deal of debate about the part the teacher should play in classroom discussion of controversial topics of the day; the suggestion is made that he ought to be neutral chairman. We have found no support at all for this view... there is all the difference in the world between letting people know where you stand in an issue and ramming your views down their throats. It is quite possible for a teacher to put forward his views about a controversial issue without dominating the discussion or coercing the participants... The teacher's opinion is an important part of the evidence but it should be subject to evaluation by the students in the same way that they assess other evidence.
>
> (Schools Council Project Environment 1975: 15–16)

Moving to the explicitly environmental context for a moment, it is simply implausible to think that the values dimension of environmental and ecological citizenship can be taught as if moral reasoning were a purely procedural affair: 'The idea that opposing views on the acceptability of, say, human-caused species extinction, can simply be laid alongside one another as preferences which different people may have or lack should be rejected' (Rawles 1998: 140). Students will expect their teachers to have a view on this question and others like it, and will not be persuaded by postures of indifference. More to the point, such postures of indifference militate against effective values education because they feign the absence of what values education demands be present: a point of view that sustains and is sustained by a 'plan for life'. Teaching ecological citizenship without examples of lived commitment to views on species extinction (either way) is like teaching mathematics without numbers.

In this section I have dealt with the third question to which I believe we need to find an affirmative answer if we are to think that liberal education systems can teach environmental and ecological citizenship effectively and legitimately. The worry was that ecological citizenship, in particular, would demand too much by way of commitment to determinate 'plans for life' to be teachable in a system committed to impartiality as far as comprehensive doctrines are concerned. I have argued, though, that liberal education systems are more likely to fall foul of their own impartiality criteria *by omission* than by the systematic and proselytizing presence of any one comprehensive doctrine. Schools in a liberal system, in other words, are more likely to stand accused of partiality by *not* teaching ecological citizenship than by it being taught in the sole and explicit service of converting all 11–18-year-olds into ecological citizen automata.

Second, I have argued that environmental and ecological citizenship curricula must embrace the full implications of the indeterminate and contested nature of ecological citizenship. There is no 'truth' to be had here, and no 'impartial' way of providing students with a range of information that can be put through the equivalent of a mental machine in order to churn out the 'right' answers. The kind of reasoning appropriate to thinking about ecological citizenship can only be done in confrontation with lived examples of partiality and commitment.

I conclude, therefore, that ecological citizenship can legitimately be taught in liberal educations systems, with the two caveats above. But even if it can, will this make a difference? Is there any evidence that citizenship education makes for better citizens, or that environmental education produces people committed to sustainable development? I can only gesture at answers to these questions, since their full treatment would require research that is beyond the remit of the present project. But the gesture seems appropriate, if only to point in the direction of work that must be done.

## Will it Work?

The answer to this question, in the English context at least, is that we do not know and we will not know for some time. As we have seen, the citizenship curriculum has only just (August 2002) come on stream and so, as David Kerr points out:

The work of the policy makers, with considerable support from practitioners, in drawing up the new Citizenship Order and framework marks the beginning rather than the end of the process of strengthening citizenship education in schools. Privately, the Advisory Group envisaged that this strengthening, bringing with it a change in the political culture of the country, would take at least ten years to achieve in practice.

(Kerr 2001: 24)

Bernard Crick himself has said that the acid test is more knowledge and more participation. To repeat:

the DfES [Department for Education and Skills] has funded a seven-year study to see if this September's 11 year olds will, by 18, know more about the political, economic, social and voluntary institutions of this country and will be more involved in community and voluntary work than at present. If the results are negative or inconclusive, then compulsion [of citizenship education] should be ended.

(Crick 2002: 19)

In the specifically environmental context, plenty of faith is invested in environmental education, especially in the way that it was taken up by Agenda 21 after the Rio summit on sustainable development in 1992, in the belief that 'Education is critical for promoting sustainable development.... It is also critical for achieving environmental and ethical awareness, values and attitudes, skills and behaviour consistent with sustainable development and for effective public participation in decision-making' (in Plant 1995: 254). But does it work? Lucas, for one, is sceptical:

There are a number of studies that show that pupil's environmental attitudes tended to be positive, except when the object of concern impinges on their own lives ... Measured attitudes toward the unlimited use of motor cars, for example, tend to be those that environmental educators would count as successful, but not when the attitude measured was concerning the pupils' attitude toward *own* use of cars ... It is as if one is always 'for' the environment until one's own freedoms are impinged upon.                                            (Lucas 1991: 37)

Civic republican and post-cosmopolitan versions of citizenship, as I described them in Chapters 2 and 3, are attempts at overcoming this self-interested response to stimuli to action. The former does so by appealing to a notion of the common good to which citizens are expected to react, and the latter does so by pointing out that justice demands that individuals act in ways that are not always in their own best interest. But, as Lucas says, the intellectual recognition of necessity is not always accompanied by the required actions. At the very least, class-based lessons need to be underpinned and informed by action-orientated experiences. In Britain, and beyond, Joy Palmer has been involved in some of the most systematic research on the effect of environmental education, and her conclusion is that 'Without doubt, the single most important category of response at all levels of data analysis . . . is experience outdoors, and particularly at a young age. The influence of parents, other close relatives, individual teachers and adults is also of paramount importance' (Palmer and Neal 1994: 8–9).

If this is right, then environmental and ecological citizenship will not be learned in the confines of the classroom—but given that these citizenships take us beyond environmental education, walks in the woods are not enough either. Ecological citizens are most likely to be created through what the French call *le vécu*, or 'lived experience'. (I mentioned this 'materialist' approach to the formation of citizens in Chapter 3.) It is no accident that the most far-reaching environmentally related movement of recent times in the United States is the environmental justice movement, founded on the lived realization that it is usually poor people who live in poor environments—and that this is true throughout the world. This fact can be taught in classrooms, but those who daily live the fact are the ones who take the pioneering political action. The education experience can, of course, mimic this reality to a degree. One way, as I suggested towards the end of a previous section, would be to involve children and young adults in real campaigns related to issues of environmental and ecological citizenship. Not only would this teach them the 'citizenship syllabus', it would also offer the best chance (in the formal educational context) of politicizing them. Politicization is never mentioned in the literature associated with the British government's citizenship syllabus, probably because while the government would like us to participate more, it would also like us to be acquiescent, and politicized individuals are politically unpredictable. I believe, though, that the citizenship syllabus is something of a Trojan horse. At both the general level, and in the more specific cases of environmental and ecological citizenship, it offers teachers and students the chance to undermine the consensus that enabled it to be designed in the first place.

## Conclusions

In Chapter 3 I characterized environmental citizenship as the claiming of environmental rights against the state in a traditionally conceived public sphere and through the political mechanisms associated with that sphere. Can this type of citizenship be taught through the citizenship curriculum that is now a statutory requirement in English secondary schools? Yes, it can. All the elements of environmental citizenship are present in the curriculum. In the same chapter I characterized ecological citizenship as the exercise of ecologically related responsibilities, nationally, internationally, and intergenerationally, rooted in justice, in both the public and private spheres. Can this type of citizenship be taught through the formal citizenship curriculum? Again, yes, it can. All the elements of ecological citizenship are present in the curriculum, too. The citizenship curriculum, in other words, offers a gift-wrapped opportunity to politicize the environment for young people. Will this opportunity be grasped? In part that depends on the will of individual teachers and individual schools. But it also depends on making the right pedagogic choices in terms of selecting what to emphasize in the curriculum, and how to teach what has been selected. My advice, for what it is worth and accompanied by the pitter-patter of angels fearfully treading, is that in a constrained timetable, ethics, justice, and fairness should take precedence over learning how to write letters to one's Member of Parliament, teachers should systematically enact their own commitment and partiality in the classroom, and the textbook should be replaced by the environmental campaign.

# Conclusion

A sheet of paper containing the following description of *Citizenship and the Environment* was found lying on a table in the Open University library in August 20__. I presume it was part of a student assignment, and I reproduce it here, in conclusion, as an accurate summary of what the book is about. The final paragraph moves from description to assessment, and I concur with the remarks made there, too.

Dobson believes that ecological citizenship is an underexplored route to environmental sustainability. His claim—unverified by any empirical evidence—is that what he calls 'ecological citizens' will have a deeper commitment to sustainability than people whose sustainable behaviour is only a response to fiscal dis/incentives. He distinguishes between environmental citizenship and ecological citizenship, and argues that while the former can be spoken of in terms of the two major traditions of citizenship—liberal and civic republican—ecological citizenship requires a new framework, which he calls 'post-cosmopolitan'.

This framework is developed in the first chapter through a critique of descriptions of globalisation that stress the 'interconnectedness' and 'interdependence' of political agents in a globalising world. Building on insights from Vandana Shiva and others, Dobson argues that the key characteristic of globalisation is its asymmetries of power and effect. These asymmetries give rise to obligations that are best not regarded as being reciprocally owed, since the capacity to inflict at-a-distance harm is possessed by 'globalising' nations and political formations only. This implies that only such nations and formations should shoulder the burdens of post-cosmopolitan obligation. Throughout the book, global warming is offered as an example of the kind of asymmetrical at-a-distance effect that engenders non-reciprocal obligation.

Two types of cosmopolitanism, as political responses to globalisation, are discussed. Dobson calls these 'dialogic' and 'distributive' cosmopolitanism, and his post-cosmopolitanism shares their commitment to a citizenship beyond the state. However, both are criticised for having a 'thin' conception of the ties that bind this putative post-national citizen community. Post-cosmopolitanism shares a focus on justice with distributive cosmopolitanism but entertains a self-consciously 'materialist' account of the citizen community, the extent of which is not given by political boundaries, as in traditional conceptions of citizenship, but rather 'produced' by actions that have a globalising character. In the ecological context, the 'space' of citizenship is described by the 'ecological footpoint', which Dobson discusses at some length in chapter 3. Throughout, Dobson is keen to distinguish the community of citizenship from the community of human beings, and this distinction carries forward into a contrast between the obligations of citizenship and more broadly humanitarian obligations. The ciphers of the Good Citizen and the Good Samaritan are deployed throughout the book to signify this distinction.

Post-cosmopolitan citizenship, and by extension ecological citizenship, overflow the framework established by liberal and civic republican citizenship in four main ways, says Dobson. First, as we observed above, the obligations with which they deal are conceived as being owed non-reciprocally. Second, while post-cosmopolitan citizenship shares the language of virtue with civic republicanism, the principal virtue (or what Dobson calls the 'first virtue') here is justice. Dobson grapples with the age-old citizenship question, first prompted by Aristotle, of which virtues are to count as citizenship virtues as opposed to more general ones. He argues that the virtues of citizenship are those that enable us to meet citizenship's obligations, and in the post-cosmopolitan context that means employing virtues that enable justice to be done. The list of 'secondary' virtues may therefore include some that are not normally associated with citizenship, such as care and compassion.

Post-cosmopolitanism's third departure from the standard architecture of citizenship is that it inhabits, says Dobson, the private as well as the public arena. This is because, first, post-cosmopolitan acts of citizenship can take place in the private arena, and second, because this arena is where some of the virtues of post-cosmopolitan citizenship are ideal-typically learnt. Examples of this private realm citizenship are offered in the ecological context in Chapter 3. Finally, post-cosmopolitan citizenship is a citizenship beyond the state, a feature it shares with cosmopolitanism, and which takes it beyond liberal and civic republican frames.

Dobson suggests that the ecological citizen's injunction in its most general form is to work towards the sustainable society. Given the way in which the objective of 'the sustainable society' is often regarded as containing surreptitious references to determinate versions of 'the good life', says Dobson, this raises the question of whether the liberal state—so determined in principle to maintain its neutrality as far as 'comprehensive doctrines' are concerned—can legitimately employ the resources of citizenship in its journey towards sustainability. Dobson discusses these issues in Chapter 4, thereby adding a commentary to the growing debate on whether liberalism and sustainability are compatible. He is more optimistic in this regard than one might have suspected, especially as he takes the difficult route to compatibility by accepting at face value, as he does, liberalism's 'good life' neutrality. There is a sting in the tail, though, since Dobson's argument seems to suggest that liberalism's neutrality commits it to strong forms of sustainability—not at all the territory it is normally recognised as inhabiting.

This debate continues in Chapter 5 where Dobson considers one aspect of the 'creation' of citizens—through the state's formal education system. Where liberal states offer citizenship classes, can they try to foment ecological citizens without falling foul of the self-imposed neutrality rule? Dobson explores this question through an examination of the newly-installed compulsory citizenship part of England's national curriculum for secondary (high) schools. Once again he comes to the conclusion that this curriculum offers ample opportunity to teach ecological citizenship, and that doing so need not bring liberalism into value-driven conflict with itself. But just as Chapter 4's optimism involved an immanent critique of liberalism, so Dobson argues that liberalism will only remain value-neutral as far as citizenship education is concerned if, precisely, it ensures that ecological citizenship is taught with a full commitment to, and recognition of, its norm-ridden character.

A key question in assessing this book is whether post-cosmopolitan citizenship and its ecological exemplar really do constitute a 'new type' of citizenship. Cosmopolitans may feel hard done by, and both liberals and civic republicans may still lay claim to covering much of the environmental ground Dobson sketches out here. But then ecological politics are always being appropriated by someone, somewhere. Dobson's apparent support for the liberal route to sustainability will disappoint radicals of many hues, but it is important to see that this support is driven by a shape-shifting critique of liberalism that leaves its commitments looking rather different to what we might expect. The focus on citizenship itself probably underemphasizes the fantastically powerful structural obstacles to sustainability at work in the world today—although the reminder that those structures are themselves made up of individuals/citizens is timely. Finally, the belief that ecological citizenship can be 'taught', through the formal channels of a state's education system or not, stands in tension—at least—with remarks in Chapter 3 to the effect that an hour's 'lived experience' can produce more politicisation than a year in class. Or reading this book.

# References

Aarhus Convention (1998), Convention on Access to Information, Public Participation in Decision-Making and Access to Justice in Environmental Matters, http://www.unece-org/env/pp/documents/cep43e.pdf.

Alliance of Small Island States (n.d.), 'Climate Change', http://www.sidsnet.org/aosis/.

Anderson, V. (1991), *Alternative Economic Indicators*, London: Routledge.

Aristotle (1946), *The Politics (Book III)*, Oxford: Oxford University Press.

Armitage, S. (2002), 'The Convergence of the Twain', http://www.bbc.co.uk/radio4/today/reports/arts/millenniumpoem.shtml.

Arthur, J. and Wright, D. (eds.) (2001), *Teaching Citizenship in the Secondary School*, London: David Fulton Publishers.

Attfield, R. (2002), 'Global Citizenship and the Global Environment', in N. Dower and J. Williams (eds.), *Global Citizenship: A Critical Reader*, Edinburgh: Edinburgh University Press.

Barry, B. (1999), 'Sustainability and Intergenerational Justice', in A. Dobson (ed.), *Fairness and Futurity: Essays on Environmental Sustainability and Social Justice*, Oxford: Oxford University Press.

Barry, J. (1999), *Rethinking Green Politics*, London, New Delhi: Sage.

—— (2002), Vulnerability and Virtue: Democracy, Dependency, and Ecological Stewardship', in B. Minteer and Pepperman B. Taylor (eds.), *Democracy and the Claims of Nature*, Lanham, Boulder, New York, Oxford: Rowman and Littlefield.

Bauman, Z. (1998), *Globalization: The Human Consequences*, Cambridge: Polity.

Beckerman, W. and Pasek, J. (2001), *Justice, Posterity and the Environment*, Oxford: Oxford University Press.

Beckman, L. (2001), 'Virtue, Sustainability and Liberal Values', in J. Barry and M. Wissenburg (eds.), *Sustaining Liberal Democracy: Ecological Challenges and Opportunities*, Houndmills: Palgrave.

Behnke, A. (1997), 'Citizenship, Nationhood and the Production of Political Space', *Citizenship Studies*, 1/2, 243–65.

Bell, D. (2002), 'How can Political Liberals be Environmentalists?', *Political Studies*, 50/4, 703–24.

Bonnet, M. (2002), 'Education for Sustainability as a Frame of Mind', *Environmental Education Research*, 8/1, 9–20.

Breckenridge, C. *et al.* (eds.) (2002), *Cosmopolitanism*, North Carolina: Duke University Press.

Bulmer, M. and Rees, A. (1996), *Citizenship Today: The Contemporary Relevance of T. H. Marshall*, London, Pennsylvania: UCL Press.

Burchell, D. (1995), 'The Attributes of Citizens: Virtues, Manners and the Activity of Citizenship', *Economy and Society*, 24/4, 540–58.

Bush, G. (2001), 'President Bush Discusses Global Climate Change' (June), http://www.whitehouse.gov/news/releases/2001/06/2001061 1–2.html.

Cain, D. (1994), 'Mathematics', in S. Goodall (ed.), *Developing Environmental Education in the Curriculum*, London: David Fulton Publishers.

Carr, D. (1999), 'Cross questions and Crooked answers', in J. Halstead and T. McLaughlin (eds.), *Education in Morality*, London: Routledge.

Castells, M. (2001), 'The Rise of the Fourth World', in D. Held and A. McGrew, *The Global Transformations Reader: an introduction to the Globalization debate*, Cambridge: Polity.

Caney, S. (2001), 'International Distributive Justice', *Political Studies*, 49/5, 974–97.

Chambers, N., Simmons, C., and Wackernagel, M. (2000), *Sharing Nature's Interest: Ecological Footprints as an Indicator of Sustainability*, London, Stirling: Earthscan.

Cheah, P. and Robbins, B. (1998), *Cosmopolitics: Thinking and Feeling Beyond the Nation*, Minnesota: University of Minnesota Press.

Christoff, P. (1996), 'Ecological Citizens and Ecologically Guided Democracy', in B. Doherty and M. de Geus (eds.), *Democracy and Green Political Thought: Sustainability, Rights and Citizenship*, London, New York: Routledge.

Clarke, P. B. (1996), *Deep Citizenship*, London, Chicago: Pluto Press.

# References

Cohen, J. (1954), *The Principles of World Citizenship*, Oxford: Basil Blackwell.

Crick, B. (2001), 'Foreword', in J. Arthur, I. Davies, A. Wrenn, T. Haydn, and D. Kerr (eds.), *Citizenship Through Secondary History*, London: Routledge.

—— (2002), 'Should Citizenship be Taught in British Schools?', *Prospect* (September), 16–19.

Crittenden, B. (1999), 'Moral Education in a Pluralist Liberal Democracy', in J. Halstead and T. McLaughlin (eds.), *Education in Morality*, London: Routledge.

Curry, P. (2000), 'Redefining Community: Towards an Ecological Republicanism', *Biodiversity and Conservation*, 9, 1059–71.

Curtin, D. (2002), 'Ecological Citizenship', in I. Isin and B. Turner (eds.), *Handbook of Citizenship Studies*, London: Sage.

Dagger, R. (2000), 'Republican Virtue, Liberal Freedom, and the Problem of Civic Service', unpublished paper.

Dahrendorf, R. (1994), 'The Changing Quality of Citizenship', in B. van Steenbergen (ed.), *The Condition of Citizenship*, London: Sage.

Dean, H. (2001), 'Green Citizenship', *Social Policy and Administration*, 35/5, 490–505.

Delanty, G. (2000), *Citizenship in a Global Age: Society, Culture and Politics*, Buckingham, Philadelphia: Open University Press.

Department for Education and Employment and the Qualifications and Curriculum Authority (1999), *The National Curriculum for England: Citizenship*, London: Department for Education and Employment and the Qualifications and Curriculum Authority.

Department for Environment, Food & Rural Affairs (DEFRA) (2000), *The Government's Response to the Royal Commission on Environmental Pollution's 21st Report*, http://www.defra.gov.uk/environment/rcep/21/index.htm.

Dobson, A. (1998), *Justice and the Environment: Conceptions of Environmental Sustainability and Dimensions of Social Justice*, Oxford: Oxford University Press.

—— (2000a), *Green Political Thought* (3rd edn.), London, New York: Routledge.

—— (2000b). 'Ecological Citizenship: A Disruptive Influence?', in C. Pierson and S. Tormey (eds.), *Politics at the Edge: the PSA*

*Yearbook 1999*, Houndmills, Basingstoke, New York: St. Martin's Press.

Dower, N. (2002), 'Global Ethics and Global Citizenship', in N. Dower and J. Williams (eds.), *Global Citizenship: A Critical Reader*, Edinburgh: Edinburgh University Press.

—— and Williams, J. (eds.) (2002), *Global Citizenship: A Critical Reader*, Edinburgh: Edinburgh University Press.

Dowie, M. (1995), *Losing Ground: American Environmentalism at the Close of the Twentieth Century*, Cambridge: MIT Press.

Duffell, I. (1994), 'Finance', in S. Goodall (ed.), *Developing Environmental Education in the Curriculum*, London: David Fulton Publishers.

Education for Sustainable Development (1999), http://www.nc.uk.net/ esd/.

Environmental News Network (1999), 'Small Island States Meet Over Rising Sea Levels', http://www.enn.com/enn-news-archive/1999/07/071499/smallislands_4336.asp.

Falk, R. (1994), 'The Making of Global Citizenship', in B. van Steenbergen (ed.), *The Condition of Citizenship*, London: Sage.

—— (2002), 'An Emergent Matrix of Citizenship: Complex, Uneven, and Fluid', in N. Dower and J. Williams (eds.), *Global Citizenship: A Critical Reader*, Edinburgh: Edinburgh University Press.

Flew, A. (2000), *Education for Citizenship*, London: IEA.

Fox, W. (1986), *Approaching Deep Ecology: A Response to Richard Sylvan's Critique of Deep Ecology*, Tasmania: University of Tasmania.

Fraser, N. and Gordon, L. (1994), 'Civil Citizenship Against Social Citizenship? On the Ideology of Contract-versus-charity', in B. van Steenbergen (ed.), *The Condition of Citizenship*, London: Sage.

Giddens, A. (1998), *The Third Way: The Renewal of Social Democracy*, Cambridge: Polity.

Goodall, S. (ed.) (1994), 'Introduction—Environmental Education', *Developing Environmental Education in the Curriculum*, London: David Fulton Publishers.

Gutman, A. (1995), 'Civic Education and Social Diversity', *Ethics*, 105/3, 557–79.

Harris, P. (1999), 'Public Welfare and Liberal Governance', in *Poststructuralism, Citizenship and Social Policy*, London: Routledge.

# References

Hayward, T. (2000), 'Constitutional Environmental Rights: A Case for Political Analysis', *Political Studies*, 48/3, 558–72.

—— (2001), 'Constitutional Environmental Rights and Liberal Democracy', in J. Barry and M. Wissenburg (eds.), *Sustaining Liberal Democracy: Ecological Challenges and Opportunities*, Houndmills: Palgrave.

—— (2002), 'Environmental Rights as Democratic Rights', in B. Minteer and Pepperman B. Taylor (eds.), *Democracy and the Claims of Nature*, Lanham, Boulder, New York, Oxford: Rowman and Littlefield.

Heater, D. (1999), *What is Citizenship?*, Cambridge: Polity Press.

Held, D. (2002), 'Globalization, Corporate Practice and Cosmopolitan Social Standards', *Contemporary Political Theory*, 1/1, 59–78.

Hofrichter, R. (ed.) (1994), *Toxic Struggles: The Theory and Practice of Environmental Justice*, Philadelphia: New Society Publishers.

Holden, B. (2002), *Democracy and Global Warming*, London, New York: Continuum.

Holland, A. (1999), 'Sustainability: Should We Start From Here?', in A. Dobson (ed.), *Fairness and Futurity: Essays on Environmental Sustainability and Social Justice*, Oxford: Oxford University Press.

Honohan, I. (2001), 'Friends, Strangers or Countrymen? The Ties between Citizens as Colleagues', *Political Studies*, 49/1, 51–69.

Hutchings, K. (1996), 'The Idea of International Citizenship', in B. Holden (ed.), *The Ethical Dimensions of Global Change*, Houndmills, New York: Macmillan Press and St. Martin's Press.

—— (2002), 'Feminism and Global Citizenship', in N. Dower and J. Williams (eds.), *Global Citizenship: A Critical Reader*, Edinburgh: Edinburgh University Press.

Ignatieff, M. (1991), 'Citizenship and Moral Narcissism', in Geoff Andrews (ed.), *Citizenship*, London: Lawrence and Wishart.

—— (1995), 'The Myth of Citizenship', in R. Beiner (ed.), *Theorizing Citizenship*, Albany: State University of New York Press.

Jacks, L. P. (n.d.), *Constructive Citizenship*, London: Hodder and Stoughton.

Jarvis, T. (1994), 'Design and Technology', in S. Goodall (ed.), *Developing Environmental Education in the Curriculum*, London: David Fulton Publishers.

Jelin, E. (2000), 'Towards a Global Environmental Citizenship', *Citizenship Studies*, 4/1, 47–64.

Jickling, B. and Spork, H. (1999), 'Education for the Environment: A Critique', *Environmental Education Research*, 4/3, 309–28.

Jonathan, R. (1999), 'Agency and Contingency in Moral Development and Education', in J. Halstead and T. McLaughlin (eds.), *Education in Morality*, London: Routledge.

Jones, C. (1999), *Global Justice: Defending Cosmopolitanism*, Oxford: Oxford University Press.

Jones, K. (1998), 'Citizenship in a Woman-Friendly Polity', in G. Shafir (ed.), *The Citizenship Debates: A Reader*, London, Minneapolis: University of Minnesota Press.

Kerr, D. (2001), 'Citizenship Education and Educational Policy Making', in J. Arthur, I. Davies, A. Wrenn, T. Haydn, and D. Kerr (eds.), *Citizenship Through Secondary History*, London: Routledge.

Kymlicka, W. (1999), 'Education for Citizenship', in J. Halstead and T. McLaughlin (eds.), *Education in Morality*, London: Routledge.

——and Norman, W. (1994), 'Return of the Citizen', *Ethics*, 104/January, 352–81.

Lichtenberg, Judith (1981), 'National Boundaries and Moral Boundaries: A Cosmopolitan View', in Peter Brown and Henry Shue (eds.), *Boundaries: National Autonomy and its Limits*, New Jersey: Rowman and Littlefield.

Light, A. (2002), 'Restoring Ecological Citizenship', in B. Minteer and Pepperman B. Taylor (eds.), *Democracy and the Claims of Nature*, Lanham, Boulder, New York, Oxford: Rowman and Littlefield.

Linklater, A. (1998*a*). *The Transformation of Political Community: Ethical Foundations of the Post-Westphalian Era*, Cambridge: Polity.

——(1998*b*), 'Cosmopolitan Citizenship', *Citizenship Studies*, 2/1, 23–41.

——(2002), 'Cosmopolitan Citizenship', in E. Isin and B. Turner (eds.), *Handbook of Citizenship Studies*, London: Sage.

Lister, R. (1991), 'Citizenship Engendered', *Critical Social Policy*, 32/Autumn, 65–71.

——(1995), 'Dilemmas in Engendering Citizenship', *Economy and Society*, 24/1, 1–40.

——(1997), *Citizenship: Feminist Perspectives*, Basingstoke: Macmillan Press.

# References

Lucas, A. M. (1991), 'Environmental Education: What is it, for whom, for what purpose, and how?', in S. Keiny and U. Zoller (eds.), *Conceptual Issues in Environmental Education*, New York: Peter Lang.

Marshall, T. H. (1950), *Citizenship and Social Class and Other Essays*, Cambridge: Cambridge University Press.

McCulloch, R. (1994), 'English', in S. Goodall (ed.), *Developing Environmental Education in the Curriculum*, London: David Fulton Publishers.

Meadows, D. H., Meadows, D. L., Randers, J., and Behrens III, W. (1974), *The Limits to Growth*, London: Pan Books.

Midgely, M. (1995), 'Duties Concerning Islands', in R. Elliott (ed.), *Environmental Ethics*, Oxford: Oxford University Press.

Miller, D. (2002), 'The Left, the Nation-State and European Citizenship', in N. Dower and J. Williams (eds.), *Global Citizenship: A Critical Reader*, Edinburgh: Edinburgh University Press.

Moss, J. (2001), 'Series Editor's Preface', in J. Arthur, I. Davies, A. Wrenn, T. Haydn, and D. Kerr (eds.), *Citizenship Through Secondary History*, London: Routledge.

Mulgan, G. (1991), 'Citizens and Responsibilities', in G. Andrews (ed.), *Citizenship*, London: Lawrence and Wishart.

Nisbet, R. (1974), 'Citizenship: Two Traditions', *Social Research*, 41/4, 612–37.

Norton, B. (1991), *Toward Unity Among Environmentalists*, New York, Oxford: Oxford University Press.

Norton, B. (1999), 'Ecology and Opportunity: Intergenerational Equity and Sustainable Options', in A. Dobson (ed.), *Fairness and Futurity: Essays on Environmental Sustainability and Social Justice*, Oxford: Oxford University Press.

Palmer, J. and Neal, P. (1994), *The Handbook of Environmental Education*, London, New York: Routledge.

Phillips, A. (1991), 'Citizenship and Feminist Theory', in G. Andrews (ed.), *Citizenship*, London: Lawrence and Wishart.

Plant, R. (1991), 'Social Rights and the Reconstruction of Welfare', in G. Andrews (ed.), *Citizenship*, London: Lawrence and Wishart.

Plant, M. (1995), 'The Riddle of Sustainable Development and the Role of Environmental Education', *Environmental Education Research*, 1/3, 253–66.

# References

Pocock, J. G. A. (1995), 'The Ideal of Citizenship Since Classical Times', in Ronald Beiner (ed.), *Theorizing Citizenship*, Albany: State University of New York Press.

Potter, I. (2001), 'Implementing Citizenship Education: A Curriculum Case Study', in J. Arthur and D. Wright (eds.), *Teaching Citizenship in the Secondary School*, London: David Fulton Publishers.

Preston, C. (2002), 'Animality and Morality: Human Reason as an Animal Activity', *Environmental Values*, 11/4, 427–42.

Prokhovnik, R. (1998), 'Public and Private Citizenship: From Gender Invisibility to Feminist Inclusiveness', *Feminist Review*, 60, 84–104.

Publido, L. (1996), *Environmentalism and Economic Justice*, Tucson: University of Arizona Press.

Qualifications and Curriculum Authority (1998), *Education for Citizenship and the Teaching of Democracy in Schools*, (London: QCA).

Rawles, K. (1998), 'Philosophy and the Environmental Movement', in D. Cooper and J. Palmer (eds.), *Spirit of the Environment: Religion, Value and Environmental Concern*, London: Routledge.

Rees, A. M. (1995), 'The Promise of Social Citizenship', *Policy and Politics*, 23/4, 31–325.

——(1996), 'T. H. Marshall and the Progress of Citizenship', in M. Bulmer and A. M. Rees (eds.), *Citizenship Today: The Contemporary Relevance of T. H. Marshall*, London, Pennsylvania: UCL Press.

Reid, B. and Taylor, B. (2000), 'Embodying Ecological Citizenship: Rethinking the Politics of Grassroots Globalization in the United States', *Alternatives*, 25/4, 439–66.

Reisenberg, P. (1992), *Citizenship in the Western Tradition: Plato to Rousseau*, Chapel Hill, London: University of North Carolina Press.

Roche, M. (1987), 'Citizenship, social theory and social change', *Theory and Society*, 16/3, 363–99.

——(1992), *Rethinking Citizenship: Welfare, Ideology and Change in Modern Society*, Cambridge: Polity Press.

——(1995), 'Citizenship and Modernity', *The British Journal of Sociology*, 46/4, 715–33.

Royal Society, The (1998), *Genetically Modified Plants for Food use and Human Health—An Update*, London: Royal Society.

Sagoff, M. (1988), *The Economy of the Earth: Philosophy, Law and the Environment*, Cambridge: Cambridge University Press.

# References

Schlosberg, D. (1999), *Environmental Justice and the New Pluralism*, Oxford: Oxford University Press.

Schools Council Project Environment (1974), *Education for the Environment*, London: Longman Group.

—— (1975), *Ethics and Environment*, London: Longman Group.

Sevenhuijesen, S. (1998), *Citizenship and the Ethics of Care: Feminist Considerations on Justice, Morality and Care*, London: Routledge.

Shafir, G. (ed.), (1998), 'Introduction: The Evolving Tradition of Citizenship', in *The Citizenship Debates: A Reader*, London, Minneapolis: University of Minnesota Press.

Shelton, D. (1991), 'Human Rights, Environmental Rights, and the Right to Environment', *Stanford Journal of International Law*, 28, 103–38.

Shiva, Vandana (1998), 'The Greening of Global Reach', in Gearóid O. Thuatail, Simon Dalby, and Paul Routledge (eds.), *The Geopolitics Reader*, London: Routledge.

Smith, G. (2004), 'Liberal Democracy and the "Shaping" of Environmentally-enlightened citizens', in Wissenburg and Y. Levy (eds.), *Liberal Democracy and Environmentalism: The End of Environmentalism?*, London: Routledge.

Smith, M. (1998), *Ecologism: Towards Ecological Citizenship*, Buckingham: Open University Press.

Somers, M. (1994), 'Rights, Relationality and Membership: Rethinking the Making and Meaning of Citizenship', *Law and Social Enquiry*, 19/1, 63–112.

Stephens, P. (2001*a*), 'Green Liberalisms: Nature, Agency and the Good', *Environmental Politics*, 10/3, 1–22.

—— (2001*b*). 'The Green Only Blooms Amid the Milllian Flowers: A Reply to Marcel Wissenburg', *Environmental Politics*, 10/3, 43–7.

Steward, F. (1991), 'Citizens of Planet Earth', in G. Andrews (ed.), *Citizenship*, London: Lawrence and Wishart.

Stewart, A. (1995), 'Two Conceptions of Citizenship', *The British Journal of Sociology*, 46/1, 63–78.

Strategy Unit, The (2002), *Waste Not, Want Not: A Strategy for Reducing the Waste Problem in England*, London: Cabinet Office, http://www.cabinet-office.gov.uk/innovation/2002/waste/report_menu.shtml.

Sylvan, R. and Bennett, D. (1994), *The Greening of Ethics: From Human Chauvinism to Deep-green Theory*, Cambridge: The White Horse Press.

Szasz, A. (1994), *Ecopopulism: Toxic Waste and the Movement for Environmental Justice*, Minneapolis: University of Minnesota Press.

Taylor, A. (1992), *Choosing Our Future: A Practical Politics of the Environment*, London: Routledge.

Taylor, B. (ed.) (1995), *Ecological Resistance Movements: The Global Emergence of Radical and Popular Environmentalism*, New York: SUNY Press.

Teachers' Guide—National Curriculum (2002), http://www.standards.dfes.gov.uk/pdf/secondaryschemes/cit_guide.pdf.

Turner, B. (1986), 'Personhood and Citizenship', *Theory, Culture and Society*, 3/1, 1–16.

—— (1990), 'A Theory of Citizenship', *Sociology*, 24/2, 189–217.

—— (ed.) (1993a), 'Preface', *Citizenship and Social Theory*, London: Sage.

—— (ed.) (1993b), 'Contemporary Problems in the Theory of Citizenship', *Citizenship and Social Theory*, London: Sage.

—— (1994), 'Postmodern culture/Modern citizens', in B. van Steenbergen (ed.), *The Condition of Citizenship*, London: Sage.

Twine, F. (1994), *Citizenship and Social Rights: The Interdependence of Self and Society*, London: Sage.

UK Government (2002), *Sustainable Development Objectives*, http://www.sustainable-development.gov.uk/what_is_sd/object.htm.

Valencia, A. (2002), 'Ciudadanía y teoría política verde: hacia una arquitectura conceptual propia', in M. Alcántara Sáez (ed.), *Política en América Latina*, Salamanca: Ediciones Universidad de Salamanca.

van Gunsteren, H. (1994), 'Four Conceptions of Citizenship', in B. van Steenbergen (ed.), *The Condition of Citizenship*, London: Sage.

van Steenbergen, B. (ed.) (1994a), 'The condition of citizenship: an introduction', *The Condition of Citizenship*, London: Sage.

—— (ed.) (1994b), 'Towards a Global Ecological Citizen', *The Condition of Citizenship*, London: Sage.

Voet, R. (1998), *Feminism and Citizenship*, London: Sage.

Wackernagel, M. and Rees, W. (1996), *Our Ecological Footprint: Reducing Human Impact on the Earth*, British Columbia: New Society Publishers.

# References

Waks, L. (1996), 'Environmental Claims and Citizen Rights', *Environmental Ethics*, 18/2, 133–48.

Walzer, M. (1989), 'Citizenship', in T. Ball, J. Farr, and R. Hanson (eds.), *Political Innovation and Conceptual Change*, Cambridge: Cambridge University Press.

Werbner, P. (1999), 'Political Motherhood and the Feminisation of Citizenship: Women's Activism and the Transformation of the Public Sphere', in P. Werbner and N. Yuval-Davis (eds.), *Women, Citizenship and Difference*, London, New York: Zed Books.

——and Yuval-Davis, N. (1999), 'Women and the New Discourse of Citizenship', in P. Werbner and N. Yuval-Davis (eds.), *Women, Citizenship and Difference*, London, New York: Zed Books.

Wheeler, K. (1975), 'The Genesis of Environmental Education', in G. Martin and K. Wheeler (eds.), *Insights into Environmental Education*, Edinburgh: Oliver and Boyd.

Whitebrook, M. (2002), 'Compassion as a Political Virtue', *Political Studies*, 50/3, 529–44.

Wissenburg, M. (1998), *Green Liberalism: The Free and the Green Society*, London: Taylor and Francis.

—— (2001), 'Liberalism is Always Greener on the Other Side of Mill: A Reply to Piers Stephens', *Environmental Politics*, 10/3, 23–42.

World Commission on Environment and Development (1987), *Our Common Future*, Oxford, New York: Oxford University Press.

# Index

# Index

# Index